ISSN 0034-4087

RELIGIOUS EDUCATION
Volume 83
Number 2
Spring 1988

CONTENTS

EDITORIAL

The focus of this issue of *Religious Education* is on the teaching of sexual responsibility and ethical decision-making through an exploration of the moral problems related to the AIDS pandemic.

The authors of our symposium were asked to wrestle with the following questions: What is the relationship between our religious commitments and the teaching of sexual activity? What should we teach, in religious settings, about such issues as physical relationships, celibacy, promiscuity, homosexuality, prophylactic devices, determining sexual norms in our society, truth-telling in intimate relationships, using human beings for experimental drugs in trying to solve a global emergency, and the right of privacy?

Furthermore, is it possible to develop, within a religious framework, a sexual moral code that will protect individuals from sexually transmitted disease and, possibly, death? If so, what would be the contents of such a code? Can the code be derived from our religious traditions?

There are few issues as morally urgent as this one for *Religious Education* to confront. It is so tempting simply to turn away and let others deal with the growing tragedy. But, as Dr. McCarthy says at the end of his article, "failure to act could lead directly to death." It is our problem, and I am proud that the journal deals with it through the essays to follow. — *Jack D. Spiro*, Editor

TOWARD GREATER RELIGIOUS PARTICIPATION IN THE STRUGGLE TO COMBAT AIDS

Charles R. McCarthy

National Institutes of Health
Bethesda, Maryland

It is my profound belief that churches must get out of the way and encourage sexually explicit instruction that takes seriously peoples' needs for intimacy. . . . I would also say that the churches and synagogues, after cleaning up their own house — and maybe in the process of cleaning up their own house — are in fact a resource for educating people in this society [about AIDS]; and should not be written off; and should be in fact at the educational task which — as the word "rabbi" would tell you — is basically the task of the church.[1]

AIDS (Acquired Immunodeficiency Syndrome) patients and carriers of the AIDS virus (human immunodeficiency virus — HIV) are modern day equivalents of lepers in biblical times. The vast majority of AIDS sufferers in the United States are homosexual or bisexual males (66 percent), heterosexual intravenous (IV) drug users (16 percent), and homosexual or bisexual males with a history of IV drug use (8 percent).[2] Homosexual acts are illegal in 29 states, and IV drug abuse is illegal across the country. Hundreds of discrimination cases brought by AIDS patients or persons infected with AIDS virus are currently before the courts. These cases include job discrimination, housing discrimination,

---

[1] Rev. Joan Campbell, Executive Director, U.S. Office of the World Council of Churches — Address to III International Conference on AIDS, Washington, DC, June 4, 1987.

[2] *Report on the Current Status of AIDS in the United States, AIDS Update*, the United States Public Health Service, July 29, 1987.

refusal to admit those suffering from AIDS to churches and schools, exclusion from clubs and social organizations, recommendations for permanent quarantine of HIV-infected individuals, and refusal to provide or pay for medical care for AIDS patients.

Dr. Jonathan Mann of the World Health Organization made the following observation during the third International Conference on AIDS: "A global epidemic has entered a stage in which prejudice about race, about religion, and about social class and about nationality is spreading as fast as the virus itself."[3] If the churches and synagogues of this country are, as they profess to be, concerned for the rights and welfare of the estranged, the poor, the outcast, the desperate, and the ill, then they must take an active role in preventing the spread of AIDS, caring for those suffering from AIDS, counseling those at risk of AIDS, and influencing the public policy of the society that somehow must cope with AIDS.

This article will attempt to make three points: (1) the dimensions of the AIDS pandemic are staggering; (2) the churches and synagogues of this country must exercise leadership and example in reaching out to patients and their loved ones whose lives have been shattered by AIDS and in educating the public in a way that will prevent or at least slow the progress of AIDS; and (3) private, corporate, and government agencies must cooperate in an effort to mobilize resources to combat the disease and to reduce its tragic effects.

(1) *The Dimensions of the AIDS Pandemic.* Between June 1981 and July 1987, according to figures released by the Centers for Disease Control (CDC) in Atlanta in July 1987, a total of 39,263 AIDS cases were identified in the U.S. Of these, 15,615, or about 40 percent, were reported in the past 12 months. About 25 percent of the total number of AIDS cases were black and 13 percent were Hispanic.[4]

Conservative projections for the year 1991 indicate that 145,000 cases of AIDS will require medical attention, and 54,000 deaths will occur, bringing the total number of deaths in the U.S. for the decade 1982-91 to nearly 180,000 persons. That number is

---

[3] Dr. Jonathan Mann, World Health Organization — Address to III International Conference on AIDS, Washington, DC, June 2, 1987.

[4] *Report on the Current Status of AIDS in the United States, AIDS Update,* the United States Public Health Service, July 29, 1987.

about three times greater than the total number of deaths suffered by Americans in the Vietnam War.[5]

At present, the CDC estimates that there may be as many as 1.5 million Americans infected with HIV. Some estimates range as high as 1.75 million. Scientists predict that up to 30 percent of infected persons will develop AIDS within five years after diagnosis. No one knows how many infected persons will ultimately develop full-blown AIDS. It is known that the average AIDS patient lives one year after diagnosis, and nearly 90 percent of AIDS patients die within three years after diagnosis.

On a worldwide basis, estimates place the number of infected persons well beyond five million, although these are based on less reliable data. Perhaps the highest prevalence of AIDS can be found in equatorial Africa, 12 nations with 100 million people. The World Health Organization believes that several million equatorial Africans are infected by AIDS — as many as one in ten sexually active adults. The numbers of AIDS patients already dead or dying may exceed hundreds of thousands. There is at present no blood screening program in Africa. Many hospitals appear to spread the disease by use of contaminated needles. (The World Bank routinely provides its African staff members with sterile syringes in case they require an injection.) The disease in Africa seems to have spread to women in nearly equal numbers as men through heterosexual contacts. AIDS seems to be spreading unchecked through countries already plagued by poverty, famine, political instability, and absence of even rudimentary public health safeguards.[6]

At present, there is no known cure for AIDS, although several drugs have been effective in prolonging the lives of some patients. Several vaccines against the disease are currently being cautiously tested in the U.S. Even if one or more of the vaccines ultimately proves to be effective, it may take research investigators up to ten years to demonstrate its effectiveness, perfect it, and bring it to the point where it can be widely used.

The outlook is grim for persons infected with HIV. The outlook is grim for understaffed and overworked providers of health care for AIDS patients. The outlook is grim for the health insur-

---

[5] *Washington Post*, November 11, 1987, reported more than 58,000 names have been inscribed on the Vietnam Memorial commemorating Americans killed in the Vietnam War.

[6] *San Francisco Chronicle*, Tuesday, October 6, 1987.

ance industry and for government insurance programs in the U.S. and other countries.

The following chilling statistics have been published by the U.S. Public Health Service:[7]

Background:

— AIDS cases first reported in June 1981.
— 39,263 cases as of July 27, 1987; 22,548 known dead.
— Estimated 1.5 million Americans now infected with the AIDS virus.
— More than 270,000 cumulative cases of AIDS projected by the end of 1991 (most will come from people already infected), with more than 179,000 cumulative deaths.
— In the five-year period covered by fiscal years 1982 through 1986, the Public Health Service (PHS) committed more than $438 million to fight AIDS. PHS-AIDS expenditures for FY 1987 alone are expected to total $494.1 million. For FY 1988, the President has asked Congress to appropriate $791.3 million for PHS-AIDS initiatives.

Modes of Transmission:

— Intimate sexual contact.
— Needle-sharing among intravenous drug users.
— Infected blood and blood products.
— Infected mothers to newborns.
— No documented transmission through casual contact or by insects.

Transmission Categories — Adult/adolescent cases (13 years of age and above):

— Homosexual/bisexual men (66%)
— Intravenous drug users (16%)
— Homosexual/bisexual men with history of intravenous drug use (8%)
— Hemophilia/coagulation disorder (1%)
— Heterosexual transmission (4%)
— Transfusion, blood/blood components (2%)
— Undetermined (3%)

2. *What the Churches and Synagogues Can Do*. At the third International Conference on AIDS held in Washington, D.C. in June, Mr. Justice Michael Kirby of Australia, himself a devout Anglican, observed that the U.S. is "too religious" to mount the kind of education program necessary to combat the spread of AIDS.[8]

Kirby did not fully explain his observation. Perhaps he meant that it is easier for religious bodies in this country to engage in

---

[7] *Report on the Current Status of AIDS in the United States, AIDS Update*, the United States Public Health Service, July 29, 1987.

[8] Mr. Justice Michael Kirby, Court of Appeals, New South Wales, Australia — Address to the III International Conference on AIDS, Washington, DC, June 2, 1987.

condemnation of sinners and pronouncements that state or imply that AIDS is God's judgment on homosexuals and IV drug abusers than to combat the disease and comfort those afflicted by it. Such a position could allow the smug and the arrogant to align themselves safely on the side of God while doing little or nothing to address AIDS as a disease. Once it is admitted that AIDS is a disease like other diseases, then AIDS must be addressed with charity and justice at the level of the individual as well as at every level of society.

Rev. Joan Campbell stated the case bluntly at the third International Conference on AIDS: "We know too well from reading history [that regarding disease as judgment] creates an atmosphere in which scapegoating is an easy response and stigmatizing, isolation, and ostracization are inevitable. Death can then be accompanied by rejection, and this becomes the most painful symptom of all."[9]

Instead of condemning HIV-infected persons as pariahs, the churches and synagogues have an opportunity to preach, teach, and practice mercy and compassion rather than judgment and punishment. Preaching and teaching will be effective only to the extent that faith communities serve the sick and the dying in effective, professional, and compassionate service. Unless service is genuine and unreserved, the religious bodies may well be subject to the criticism of hypocrisy.

Service to the sick and the dying is desperately needed, but it is not enough to meet the challenge of AIDS. As noted above, it is probable that 1.5 million Americans are infected with HIV. Public policy-makers are struggling with the issues associated with the question of which segments of society should be tested for AIDS and whether the tests should be mandatory or voluntary. The churches and synagogues are in an excellent position to advocate for appropriate testing and to mediate the conflict between the privacy rights of individuals and the public health rights of society. Such advocacy and mediation will require careful study, diplomacy, statesmanship above partisan politics, and dispassionate judgment. No group in our society is as well positioned to play this role as the churches and synagogues. An ecumenical effort is called for.

All experts agree that testing for presence of the HIV is, in and

---

[9] Rev. Joan Campbell, Executive Director, U.S. Office of the World Council of Churches — Address to III International Conference on AIDS, June 4, 1987.

of itself, of little value. Testing accompanied by appropriate counseling is what is needed. Yet trained counselors, willing to work in drug addiction treatment centers, in sexually-transmitted disease clinics, and in institutions established and operated by the gay community, are in short supply. Are the churches and synagogues willing to recruit, train, subsidize, and provide support systems for desperately needed counselors to work in areas that are found at the margins of our society? Perhaps no societal resource is so lacking. Are the faith communities ready and willing to supply this resource?

3. *The Public Sector.* The imperative of service demands that churches and synagogues use their influence, not only in providing personal service for the sick and counseling the afflicted but in directing and re-directing corporate and public resources to provide increased dollars for research, special care facilities for the sick and dying, an actuarial base for health insurance, and training for caregivers at every level.

Although drugs that prolong the lives of at least some afflicted persons (and vaccines that may one day prevent or slow the progress of AIDS) are currently being developed and tested, the probability of finding a cure or an effective vaccine in the next few years is small. If prevention is to be effective in the meantime, it must come through the kind of education that produces a change in behavior. Here is a role in which the churches and synagogues have the best record of any instrument in our society. To date, little of the educational potential of religious bodies has been actualized.

Teaching is central to faith communities. Education of the whole person and formation of right attitudes and other-regarding motivation have always been goals of religious education. Churches and synagogues are often more successful than any other agents in our society in attaining these goals. Few issues fall within the avowed goals of religious bodies as clearly as education concerning AIDS and AIDS prevention. The fragility of life, the meaning of death, the human need for intimacy, the centrality of sex in personhood, the consequences of human behavior, the choice of lifestyle, respect for the privacy and integrity of others, the power of good example, and the support of community are traditional religious values. The value of chastity or (failing chastity) the obligation to reduce risks to oneself and others, comforting the afflicted, identification and condemnation of discrimination, the need for service even at some personal risk, and the value of prayer and trust in God are traditional components of religious education. They are also central to a right attitude toward AIDS.

Religious bodies are already well organized and capable of presenting such teaching. To do so will require courage and leadership by church leaders. Kirby, in a moment of pessimism, has stated that America is "too religious" (in a pejorative sense of the word) to meet the challenge of AIDS. But in a more optimistic mood he has called on all "educated and thoughtful people . . . to go back to our communities and spread the gospel of compassion and understanding. If we are scientists we have to redouble our efforts to find cures, if we are lawyers or social scientists we have to redouble our efforts to find the cure to panic."[10] He might well have added, If we are ministers or rabbis, religious teachers, or members of the laity we must teach our people to care for victims, to comfort the afflicted to prevent tragedy, to administer justice, and to mobilize all available resources in dealing with the pandemic of AIDS.

So far the religious bodies in this country have been cautious and timid in reaching out to the gay community, in supporting the IV drug addiction community, in educating the young about the dangers of unsafe sex, in preventing the spread of AIDS, and in caring for the oppressed, the frightened, and the sick. The time has come to embrace modern-day lepers and transform them by justice and charity into persons who command and receive dignity and respect. Failure to act could lead directly to death — death that could have been prevented.

Dr. McCarthy is director of the Office for Protection from Research Risks, National Institutes of Health. He has served on numerous ethics committees concerned with the rights and welfare of AIDS patients.

The views expressed in this article are those of the author and do not reflect the position of any component of the Federal Government.

---

[10] Mr. Justice Michael Kirby, Court of Appeals, New South Wales, Australia — Address to III International Conference on AIDS, June 4, 1987.

BEARING ONE ANOTHER'S BURDENS

Abigail Rian Evans

Georgetown University
Washington, D.C. 20057

An adequate response to AIDS entails an examination of theological, pastoral, ethical, medical, educational, and governmental issues. AIDS raises for us the basic questions about the relationship between sin and sickness, health and salvation, evil and a God of love, the existence of suffering, punishment and innocence, community responsibility and individual accountability, forgiveness, and restoration. Stemming from these fundamental issues are concerns about sexual ethics and education, confidentiality versus public safety, and health care practices and protection.

The AIDS crisis confronts the church and synagogue with the need to examine the relationship of God to human sickness and suffering and our response to it. The question is not simply one of sexual ethics or lifestyle, but one that strikes at the heart of our theology. As one person dying of AIDS asked me, "Why should I have contracted AIDS from one sexual encounter with the wrong person when thousands of other sexually promiscuous people are disease free?"

The current transmission of the disease makes it clear that new lovers and spouses may affect an innocent partner. An example would be the case of someone with a history of multiple sexual partners who is now reformed and secretive of his or her past and an unknown HIV positive. Hence, a restrictive sexual code will not resolve the tragedy of AIDS. It is an oversimplification to reduce the problem of AIDS to one of sexual lifestyle. Educational campaigns are mandatory, prudent behavior required, *limited* screening and quarantine recommended. These measures, however, neither exhaust the responses nor touch on the basic theological problems.

There are two principal questions I will discuss in this paper: the first concerns prevention, the second treatment. Both relate to educating people concerning AIDS.

1. Will a religiously-based sexual ethic help prevent AIDS?

2. How should we respond to the person with AIDS?

The discussion of these questions will be in the context of sexually-transmitted AIDS and only secondarily to situations where AIDS is contracted by intravenous drug users, babies of AIDS mothers, or hemophiliacs. My perspectives are drawn from the Old and New Testament scriptures and from the tenets of Reformed Theology.

Will a religiously-based sexual ethic help prevent AIDS? Before we can answer this question, we need to examine the prior question of how to motivate people to follow a religious sexual code. Motivation to follow the religious code is influenced by society's general views toward religion and God. Although 90 percent of the American public professes a belief in God, according to a recent Gallup poll, this belief is rarely translated into adherence to a religious code for sexual behavior.

There are a number of reasons why religious sexual ethics are rejected:

1. Pluralism and valuelessness of contemporary society.

The social cohesion that the Deuteronomic code developed in the Hebrew nation and the acceptance of a uniform ethical code by the Christian community no longer exist in contemporary American society. Much like the period of the Judges, "Each one does what is right in his own eyes." As Saul Bellow has expressed it, we live in an age of moral interregnum where we have used up all the old values without replacing them with new ones. If there is any dominant ethic, it is utilitarian and pragmatic and relative and situational, rather than objective and universal. Rights are emphasized over responsibilities; phrases like "a right to my own body" and "my share of the American dream" are common. They reflect a time of the righting of past injustices, but in so doing, individual rights have replaced responsibility to society and sometimes even to family and neighbor. The effect of this milieu is the absence of a larger social support for ethical codes in general and sexual ethics in particular.

2. Desire for immediate gratification rather than long-term pleasure.

Part of the extension of emphasis on rights is the belief that immediate pleasure is one's right. The open-ended relationships sought in sex mirror our general autonomy-based culture, as well as echoing the culture of narcissism that Christopher Lasch described in the 1970s. Sex is fun, so why delay the pleasure? If it is good in and of itself, why worry about the context of the sex act or its long-term consequences? The playboy philosophy, which dominates, suggests that for real sexual pleasure one should respond to the opportunities available. We note, for example, how male/female relationships are now more often described as encounters rather than relationships and even less so as life-long marriage. We are bombarded by messages of sexual freedom. Delayed pleasure is not in; peer pressure mandates otherwise.

3. Preference of romantic over married love.

In contrast to the immediate gratification view of sex is our society's romanticized version of love. As Denis de Rougement argues in his book, *Love in the Western World*, the absence of responsibility and commitment in love and sex in Western society can be traced to the medieval view expressed in myths such as Tristan and Isolde. This view can be described as the "cult-of-the-far-away-princess," where the pursuit of the beloved is more fascinating than her possession. Obstacles are created, such as the sword between Tristan and Isolde, to keep the lovers apart; the ultimate separation then becomes death, because an idealized love does not want actualization in this life. Underlying this view is a fear of becoming bored and disillusioned. Married love then becomes equated with boredom and contrasted with romantic love, which becomes the ideal. Once the woman is wedded and bedded, for the man she loses her fascination.

4. Negative, guilt-tinged views of sex by some religious groups.

The negative view of some religious groups toward sex alienates young people and others from a biblical view of sexual ethics. This distorted view of Reformed Theology emphasizes the need to suppress the body rather than presenting the body as a gift of God, which is the basis for enjoying sexual relations. The Gnostic strains of early church heresies still affect the Protestant understanding of human nature. In its desire to emphasize our spiritual side, it has forgotten the material creation, the incarnation, the body as the temple of the Holy Spirit, the bodily resurrection, and the sacraments that affirm the goodness of the body. Heirs of Calvin have often emphasized a more puritanical understanding of the flesh.

5. Lack of understanding about the dynamics of male/female relationships.

Contemporary views of sex are often extracted from its part in the larger schema of male/female relationships. From pre-adolescence through middle age, sex is viewed as the vehicle for popularity and acceptance. For the female, the gift of virginity is viewed as a sacrifice on the altar of popularity with males, but often the bitter truth is that, when shallowly given, it is superficially received. Women experience an ambivalence in sexual intercourse when they attempt to act liberated by "casual encounters" but often experience a longing for a deeper relationship. So, generally, while women may view sex as part of a larger relationship implying commitment and fidelity, even if for a stated period, for many men sex is a conquest without long-term obligation. Sex is literally in and out for these men. Given this superficial understanding of heterosexual relationships, there is little interest in the broader questions that a religious ethic addresses.

6. Ignorance of consequences of following unhealthy sexual practices.

Despite education about sexually transmitted diseases, large segments of the population are ignorant of routes of their transmission or prevention techniques. Educational programs about AIDS will only be effective if a desire to act on the information is present and if an understanding of the failure to pursue positive behavior is clear. For example, a poll of San Francisco teens revealed the following scattered information about AIDS: 92 percent knew AIDS was transmitted by sexual intercourse, but only 2.6 percent were aware that condoms reduced the risk of transmission; 3.68 percent knew that casual contact does not spread AIDS, and only 4.78 percent were afraid of getting AIDS.[1]

7. Sense of immunity from harmful consequences of dangerous sexual practices.

Here we note that although people may have the facts and necessary information, there is a philosophy, especially among teenagers, of being immune from the consequences of harmful behavior. For example, despite the availability of birth control and the legality of abortions, teenage pregnancies have dramatically increased (30,000 girls under age 15 and more than one million American teenagers will become pregnant per year).[2] The

---

[1] John Langone, "AIDS Update: Still No Reason for Hysteria." *Discover* (September 1986).

[2] *Time*, December 9, 1985, pp. 78-79.

lack of a realistic view of how one's actions and decisions affect one's future is not limited to adolescents.

How do we motivate for adherence to a religious sexual ethic? In light of these factors, which lead to a rejection of a religiously-based sexual ethics, we need to promote a positive view of sex that attracts rather than repels people. The desire to follow this ethic needs to be grounded, not in fear of punishment, but commitment to a positive fulfillment of human sexuality. It should provide a vision of glory, which recognizes the place of sex as part, not the whole, of God's plan for our love relationships.

Unfortunately, most of the sexual ethics to date offered in response to AIDS have been negative prohibitions rather than positive, affirming perspectives. Sloganism — condoms vs. abstinence — has replaced ethical reflection. Even Mayor Koch of New York City has entered the fray by running ads in the *New York Times* praising abstinence and warning that condoms provide *safer* sex but not *safe* sex. Sex therapists who used to counsel for open sexual relationships now encourage monogamy. They are counseling couples to seek ways to enhance their sexual relationships rather than seeking fulfillment outside of marriage.[3]

We should not predicate our whole sexual ethic on the negative injunction of abstinence. Abstinence starts from a negative prohibition rather than a positive ethic. Perhaps a starting point would be to educate toward the beauty of the mystery of sex in its slow unfolding, to suggest that intercourse is not the *sine qua non* of sexual intimacy; there are nuances of sexual expression to be experienced, which can enhance the sexual pleasure. Hence a decision for virginity, rather than being a decision against pleasure, may reflect a desire for retaining mystery and future pleasure. Too often, momentary gratification may carry the seeds of eventual sadness.

Sexual ethics should consist of more than prohibitions; they should also emphasize pleasures. We need to change the mindset that casual sex is good and, instead, link intimacy, love, sex, commitment, and marriage, which is more likely to produce meaningful relationships.

We should not develop a sexual ethic only for the AIDS tragedy, but create an ethic that applies to the whole spectrum of sexual behavior. The basic question in intimate physical relation-

---

[3] Theresa L. Crenshaw, M.D., "AIDS Update: Condoms are Not Enough," *AASECT Newsletter*, Vol. 18 (April 1987), pp. 20, 22.

ships is one of responsibility, commitment, and vulnerability. Any sexual encounter carries with it a tremendous risk of loss and pain as well as long-lasting fulfillment and joy. Sexual intercourse, even if undertaken as a purely physical act, always carries the possibility of spiritual and emotional intimacy.

For the Christian, sexual behavior is related to our understanding of how God created us as body, mind, and spirit; these parts are an integrated whole not to be severed one from another. Furthermore, we are created as male and female, complementary to one another, together completing what it means to be human.

The Old and New Testaments offer the ideal — intimate sex and love within the covenant of marriage. For example, the prophet Hosea's fidelity to Gomer, his unfaithful wife, is not only a symbol of God's relation to Israel but a paradigm for the covenant of marriage. The Genesis account of the joining of male and female who are "to know each other and to forsake all others" and "to be fruitful and multiply" gives a vision of the union of physical and spiritual love. Paul's comparison of the relation of the church and Christ to that of a husband to his wife further elevates the spiritual vision of marriage. In Ephesians 4, we note the sacrificial and self-giving side of love. In the biblical perspective, the linking of sex to love is central. When sex is severed from love, its true depth is lost, and complete intimacy is not possible.

In summary, how do we motivate people to adhere to a religious sexual ethic, which will in turn help prevent the spread of AIDS?

1. First, by teaching and inspiring individuals to accept that, in sexual relationships, long-term commitment and stability are superior to short-term hedonistic lust.

The mandate is not that we should embrace spiritual love (agape) with the purpose of concealing all physical desire, but rather that covenant love will heighten the physical pleasure of sex. As W. F. May has suggested, sex has been viewed as demonic, divine, romantic, and casual — all of which does a disservice to the Christian understanding of sex.[4]

From the Old Testament perspective, sexual intercourse was described in terms of "knowing" the beloved. So, complete union embraces the physical, emotional, mental, and spiritual — each is heightened by the other. The soaring quality of physical love is in

---

[4] William F. May, *Passionate Attachments: Thinking About Love.* (New York: Free Press, in press).

proportion to the degree of spiritual intimacy. As Paul writes in I Corinthians 13, perfect love casts out fear. So when fear and inhibition are gone, our deepest desires may be satisfied. Generally, hedonistic sex carries its own seeds of self-destruction: a frantic search for more and more bizarre forms of sex in the hope that pleasure will be forthcoming. A jaded boredom results that no number of pornographic magazines or sexual devices can assuage.

2. By emphasizing the ideal of monogamous, hetereosexual relationships as the perfect expression of physical love.

Monogamy as an ideal stems from the Judeo-Christian teaching that becoming one flesh creates a bond between a man and a woman, which is unique. If this bond is broken by unfaithfulness and/or promiscuity, sex is severed from love and commitment. Furthermore, monogamy is predicated on an understanding of God's created order as heterosexual, not homosexual. Homosexuality sits at the center of the discussion about AIDS. No matter where one stands theologically, homosexuality is a controversial and painful issue. There is probably no Christian congregation that does not have some members who are homosexual. All the major denominations have hotly debated the issue. Even when achieving a majority position opposing the homosexual lifestyle, a vocal minority continues to lift this up as an alternate. There is no doubt that there are some within the Protestant churches who view AIDS as just retribution for this sinful lifestyle, while others try to dissociate completely homosexuality and AIDS.

If we take the creation story seriously, that God created male and female to be complementary to one another and together fulfill what it means to be created in God's image and to be human, then any homosexual relationship will lack this sense of wholeness. It is another sign of our broken world, not what God meant for us — hence wrong but not unforgiveable. Surely it may be much less of a sin than, say, divorce or adultery or pedophilia. Furthermore, there are different types of homosexuality — economic, physiological, psychological, and transient. It is inappropriate to address homosexuals as one group in discussing their sexual lifestyle. For example, if conversion from homosexuality is not possible, then promoting an ethic of celibacy or monogamy within the homosexual lifestyle is important.[5]

---

[5] For example, the spread of AIDS in Haiti to a large degree is linked to poor men who had sex with homosexual tourists for purely economic reasons. See Lisa Scanzoni, *Is the Homosexual My Neighbor?*, New York: Harper & Row, 1980.

3. By placing physical love and sex within the context of other forms of love.

First, we must heed C. S. Lewis's warning against deifying physical love "when love ceases to be a demon, only when he ceases to be a God."[6] The demonic nature of eros is not in its pleasure but rather in its deification — that because of its nearness to God, its exalted nature can cause a type of idolatry, which attempts to replace God in our lives. As C. S. Lewis has suggested, there are other faces of love — charity (*agape*), affection (*storge*), and friendship (*phileo*), which complete our understanding of love.[7]

As we come to understand other forms of love, we can enjoy physical love as complementary to, not replacing, them. Human love, from the very nature of the case, is predominantly a need-love. Affection is primarily a need-love; what it needs is to give. It is a gift-love that needs to be needed. Appreciative love is a very comfortable kind of love; it lies, so to speak, curled up asleep — "no need to talk, no need to make love, no needs at all, except perhaps to stir the fire."[8] The glory of affection is that it can unite those who are most emphatically, even comically, dissimilar, but who come together despite their dissimilarities.

Friendship is another form of love, which has not been appropriately valued, especially in our culture. It is the instrument by which God reveals to us the beauty of others. We face the world together with strong bonds of kinship. Friendship between the members of the same sex is a special pleasure because there is a natural understanding of each other, which is more difficult to achieve in heterosexual relationships.

Charity or God's love is the most important face of love; this is not because it *replaces* the other loves but because it *fulfills* them. This self-giving love transforms all our other experiences of love. When we meet God, we do not lay aside all our experiences of love, because God is the one who gives us love. As we give our love to God, then God returns it to us and transforms that love in a very special way.

C. S. Lewis concludes his exposition of the four loves with these remarks: "Theologians have sometimes asked whether we will know one another in heaven and whether the particular love

---

[6] C. S. Lewis, *The Four Loves* (New York: Harcourt Brace Jovanovich, 1960), p. 17.

[7] C. S. Lewis, *The Four Loves.*

[8] C. S. Lewis, *The Four Loves*, p. 57.

relations worked out on earth will then continue to have any significance." It seems reasonable to reply, it may depend on what
kind of love had become or was becoming on earth. He concludes
by saying,

> At the end of our lives, when we were made for God, and we are mov-
> ing towards being with God, only by being in some respect like him,
> only by being a manifestation of his beauty, loving, kindness, wisdom,
> or goodness has any earthly beloved excited our love. It is not that we
> have loved them too much, but that we did not quite understand what
> we were loving. It is not that we shall be asked to turn from them so
> dearly familiar to a stranger when we stand before God. When we see
> the face of God, we shall know that we have always known it. He has
> been a party to and has made, sustained, and moved moment by mo-
> ment within all our earthly experiences of love. All that was true love in
> them was even on earth far more his than ours, and ours only because of
> his.[9]

4. By educating people toward good decision-making.

Once a positive, healthy view of sexuality has been developed,
then we need to assist people in decision-making to follow it.
First, accurate information and facts are needed to make reasonable decisions. We need to choose a course of action, then understand the consequences of those choices. In ethical decision-
making, we move from principles, to data, to situations. We need
to comprehend the forces that move us to decisions — passion,
loneliness, ignorance, fear, love, and hate — and to balance reason
and emotion.

AIDS is the ideal lab for understanding the consequences of
behavior, both immediate and long-term. Fear should not be the
motivator. It may backfire in emotional dysfunction and loss of
confidence in the future. For example, fear of nuclear war has
done this for some people. It can lead to the attitude, "Since I can't
control my future, it doesn't matter what I do."

If following the religious sexual code produces positive, transforming experiences, and disobedience brings tragedy and heart-
ache, then the motivation to follow it will obviously be enhanced.
In terms of AIDS, the first step in equipping people to choose
healthy sex (healthy here is defined in the broad sense of spiritual,
mental, and physical well-being) is to provide accurate information. Complete medical facts are essential.

Attitudinal change should be the goal of our education. The

---

[9] C. S. Lewis, *The Four Loves*, pp. 190-191.

Victorian AIDS Council in Australia has undertaken major research on attitudes towards AIDS, trying to eliminate fear as a
motivator, which seems to be the principle emotion in the U.S.
towards AIDS. In summary, a religiously-based sexual ethic can
help prevent AIDS by motivating people toward healthy sexual
behavior and providing a broader setting for sex within the context of committed love.

Now that we have addressed one approach to the prevention
of AIDS, that is, adopting an affirming attitude to sexual behavior, how do we relate to those persons who, through unhealthy
and harmful sexual acts, have contracted AIDS?

How should we respond to the person with AIDS? There has
been a tendency to put AIDS in a very special category of infectious diseases based on the predominance of this disease among
homosexuals, bisexuals, and intravenous drug users. Many persons see AIDS as a sickness resulting from sin, especially those
from certain theological positions, who claim AIDS is God's punishment for an evil lifestyle, that is, sinful behavior.

While the Old and New Testaments frequently correlate sin
and sickness, they usually do so in the context of a warning, an
admonition to avoid certain acts (sins) in order to prevent unde-
sirable consequences. Although there is certainly relevance to
warnings in the context of AIDS and acts that can lead to its infection and transmission, the issue here is one of response, after and
not before the infection.

Here Christian theology should be guided by Christ's response
to illness, which was one of healing and not of judgment. Using
this response as a guide, we should examine how the church can
best minister to the person with AIDS, to heal, if healing becomes
possible, and to make the best of the remainder of their days if
physical healing is not possible. Compassion, not judgment,
should be our response. We cannot stand over against others since
we also experience brokenness in our lives.

To educate and motivate people to accept the person with
AIDS and minister with compassion and sensitivity, we must first
develop a theology of health and sickness, then use this theology
to enhance the church as a community of acceptance, and finally
offer the resources of healing.

1. Develop a theology of health and sickness.

Until we understand the nature of health and sickness, it is
difficult to discuss AIDS or any other illness that assaults us. Part
of the unique role of the religious community is a clarification of

the fundamental questions, which AIDS introduces, as well as a foundational structure for understanding health and sickness.

2. Health as wholeness and its relation to salvation.

The unique dimension of the biblical understanding of health as wholeness can be determined by examining its relationship to the twin concept of salvation. Health and salvation are both part of God's plan for our wholeness. Physical healing *may* be a sign of God's saving care.[10] Too often we reduce health to our bodily well-being and confine salvation to the state of our soul. In the Bible, no such dualism exists. The doctrine of God's incarnation in Jesus Christ helps clarify the Christian understanding of the relationship between health and salvation. The incarnation requires an expanded notion of humankind and calls for the integration of body and spirit.

Early Christians had to fight the Gnostic influences of their day, which regarded the body as evil and required its denial in an ascetic ethic. The apostle Paul, who fought the Gnostic view, recognized the importance of a person's total being when he referred to the body as the temple of the Holy Spirit (I Cor 6:19) and set forth the doctrine of the resurrection of the body (I Cor 15:35-38).

In the biblical tradition, health and salvation are integrally connected through their common etymology signifying wholeness; Jesus's title, Saviour, also means healer. Our health depends both on our relationship to God and to others (freedom from a state of sin) and on physical reconstruction (well-being). The Hebrew word *raphah* means heal, repair, made whole: "For he (God) wounds but he binds up. He smites, but his hands heal (make whole)."[11] In the New Testament Greek, what is often translated as "well" originally was more inclusive: "If I only touch his garment I shall be made well" ($\delta\omega\theta\eta\delta o\mu\alpha\iota$, i.e., be saved).[12] Still another word, from which we get the English word hygiene, $\dot v\gamma\iota\delta\iota\mu\epsilon\iota\nu$, means not only to be in health but also carries the sense of soundness or wholeness.[13]

Health and salvation are not *equivalents* but *related* concepts. Health and salvation are both goals, but salvation includes the indispensable additional element of God's grace, which results in our faith in Jesus Christ as Lord and Saviour. According to Re-

---

[10] Granger Westburg, *Theological Roots of Wholistic Health Care* (Hinsdale, IL: Wholistic Health Centers, Inc., 1979), p. 42.

[11] Job 5:18.

[12] Matthew 9:21.

[13] 3 John 2.

formed theology, although works are the signs of salvation, neither they nor faith is the cause or basis for it. Health, on the other hand, is not gratis, nor does it necessarily result from a strong faith. It requires active responsibility on the part of the person for its fullest realization, even though it may still elude us.

Health and salvation are also distinguished by the fact that complete health always includes physical well-being, whereas salvation does not depend upon one's bodily condition. Salvation is promised in the very midst of death. Health is a statement about our relationship to the world, including the body; salvation is a statement about our relationship to God. Salvation has to do with the transcendent and ultimate; health with the physical and present. Salvation does not consist in being freed from disease or achieving society's definition of mental health. (Saviours and martyrs are notoriously labeled as mentally unbalanced.)[14] Every Christian does not enjoy robust health. The apostle Paul suffered a "thorn" in the flesh for years.[15] Timothy apparently had various health problems.[16] Epaphroditus, a colleague of Paul, was seriously ill.[17] The New Testament does not assume that vital faith in God is accompanied by physical and mental well-being.[18]

Another dimension of the relationship of health and salvation is the connection between health, forgiveness, and obedience. (I will examine the converse of this concept when analyzing the relationship between sin and sickness.) Numerous scripture passages reflect this relationship (e.g., Ex 15:26, Ps 41:3-4, Ps 103:3, Prov 3:7-8, and Prov 4:20-22).

These discussions about the relationship of health and salvation are important in light of the tendency of some to condemn patients with AIDS as deserving of eternal punishment for their "sin." The false argument goes that physical health and spiritual well-being are always linked: Hence someone with AIDS will not be saved. The easy response to this postion is to conclude that sin and sickness are totally unrelated. However, from the biblical perspective there is a complex relationship between them but not in every individual case. As we educate our church members

---

[14] J. C. McGilvray, ed. *The Quest for Health: Report of a Study Process* (Cleator Moor, England: Bethwaites Printers, 1979), p. 27.

[15] 2 Corinthians 12:7.

[16] 1 Timothy 5:23.

[17] Philippians 2:26-30.

[18] "Relation of the Christian Faith to Health," Report of the 172nd General Assembly of the United Presbyterian Church of the United States of America (Philadelphia: Office of the General Assembly, 1960), p. 25.

about the proper response to persons with AIDS, these perspectives become crucial.

3. Sickness as brokenness and its relation to sin.

Just as recognizing the relationship between health and salvation illuminates our understanding of health as wholeness, so acknowledging a connection between sin and sickness helps interpret sickness as brokenness. Both sets of concepts tell us something about the inclusive nature of health and sickness in terms of the person and his or her community.

The issue of the relationship between sin and sickness is important both theologically and existentially. Theologically, it raises the whole set of theodicy questions; existentially it involves both the patient and the healer. It touches at the heart of the sick person's questions of why he or she is ill, whether he or she will recover, and whether he or she will have any control over illness or recovery.

The biblical perspective argues that, although it is not always causal, sin and sickness interrelate. Further, God figures in the mystery of their connectedness but always to bring about ultimate goodness and health. Thus, the healer's job is not to draw theoretical relationships between them or insist on some transparent level of connection. If, through conversations with the patient, either one of them recognizes a connection, or perhaps more importantly the absence of one, this discovery should form part of the treatment. This approach may free the patient from guilt, which inhibits healing, a problem faced by patients with AIDS.

In the Old and New Testaments, sin and sickness are linked etymologically and, in certain contexts, used interchangeably. There are several different words for each of these terms. In Hebrew *chalah* means to be rubbed or worn, to be weak, sick, afflicted, or put to grief, and is related to break, defile, or wound. The Greek carries the same double meanings: κακῶζ, translated amiss, diseased, evil, miserable; δοθεγέω, to be feeble, sick, weak; κόμγω, to faint, to be sick, to be weary. Another word for sin in the New Testament, δμαρτία, which means to miss the mark, is probably related to terms such as abnormal and maladjusted. Sin and sickness have a common historical root in the form of alienation from God, self, or society.[19]

The weight of the biblical material suggests that while per-

---

[19] See James Strong, *Strong's Exhaustive Concordance* (Michigan: Associated Publishers, n.d.), for Greek and Hebrew etymologies.

sonal sin is one's own fault, sickness is not always a consequence of an individual's own thoughts or actions. As part of the human race, we suffer the consequences of fallen human nature, as well as experience the joys of being human. As we enjoy the assets of life — sun, rain, beauty, sleep, freedom — which we may not directly create or warrant, so we suffer the liabilities of life — epidemics, tornados, wars — for which we may not be directly responsible. In the case of AIDS, innocent persons may be the victims of the disease, where clearly their actions were not the reason for contracting it. Sin and sickness are not identical, because sickness may have a nonculpable dimension that sin lacks.

Does sickness result from sin? From a Judeo-Christian perspective, there are three aspects to this question: (1) an individual's responsibility for his own sickness due to his sinful nature or act; (2) God's use of sickness as a punishment for sin; and (3) the absence of a connection between them in some instances.

In relation to the first aspect, the story of the Fall describes a spiritual break between God and man, which resulted in suffering and death. According to the Genesis account, suffering in all its forms is mentioned together with death as a consequence of sin. There are obvious examples of how the misuse and abuse of one's body, the aimlessness of one's life, and the mistreatment of others can cause one's own illness, as well as affecting future generations. AIDS especially reflects this phenomenon as illustrated by babies born of mothers with AIDS, hemophiliacs, and innocent sexual partners who suffer the consequences of someone else's actions.

A number of scriptural passages attribute sickness and even death to sin or view sickness as a direct punishment from God, for example, "the afflictions of that land and the sickness with which the Lord has made it sick."[20] Numerous Old Testament passages directly correlate sickness and God's punishment. Miriam spoke against Moses and was smitten with leprosy for seven days.[21] Leprosy struck Gehazi, Elisha's servant, for his lies and greed.[22] According to the Chronicler, Uzziah's leprosy resulted from his arrogant pride.[23] Eli died because he allowed his sons to run rampant.[24]

---

[20] Deuteronomy 29:22.

[21] Numbers 12:9-10.

[22] 2 Kings 5:27.

[23] 2 Chronicles 26:19-20.

[24] 1 Samuel 3:13, 4:17-18.

Not only did the prophetic and historical writers draw a causal relationship between sin and sickness, but so did the poetical books, especially the psalmist.[25] The inclusion of the story of Job in the Jewish canon is extremely important as a corrective to the oversimplified view that all sickness was the direct result of a particular person's sin. Job's friends who voiced the theology of their day, that sickness was God's punishment for Job's sin, were proved wrong, and Job, not they, was vindicated by God.

This complexity in the relationship between sin and sickness carries forward into the New Testament. On the one hand, Jesus implies that sickness is the work of demons.[26] Sin and sickness are both regarded as works of the devil, and victory over them are signs of God's incoming kingdom. On the other hand, after healing the paralytic, Jesus tells him to sin no more lest a worse thing befall him.[27]

Paul, reflecting the Deuteronomic point of view, appears to correlate a person's sin and sickness in relation to the incorrect eating of the Lord's Supper.[28] In James 5, we read that the prayer of faith will save the sick man, and if he has committed sins, he will be forgiven (healed). Sickness here is regarded as a special opportunity to take stock, to examine oneself concerning the reasons for illness.

There are cases mentioned in the New Testament where sickness or even death was seen as a direct punishment from God. Ananias and Sapphira were struck dead, because they lied about the purchase of property.[29] Herod Agrippa I was eaten by worms, because he did not give God the glory in his reign.[30]

In the midst of these stories, which connect sin and sickness, comes the account of the man born blind. When the disciples ask, "Who sinned, this man or his parents, that he was born blind?", Jesus replies neither one but that the glory of God might be manifest. This story disturbs the pat answers, just as the story of Job questioned whether sickness is always God's will and a punishment for sin. Christ's career was one of healing, not judgment.

---

[25] See, e.g., Psalm 6:1-2, 38:3-7, 41:3-4, 103:3; Proverbs 3:7-8.

[26] Matthew 12.

[27] Luke 5:17-26.

[28] 1 Corinthians 11:29-30.

[29] Acts 5:1-11.

[30] Acts 12:23.

However, as the story of Job reflected, suffering is a mystery, but God's goodness ultimately triumphs.

AIDS should be viewed not as some special sickness singled out by God as a judgment upon certain people, but rather a further reflection of the broken world in which we live. It, like other forms of suffering, is a mystery and a tragedy, the result of a mixture of our imperfect world, our own culpability, and the tragic sense of life. The Bible does not provide a basis for concluding that homosexuality is a sin, the punishment for which consists of sickness and suffering, nor, on the other hand, does it defend a position that lifestyle choices never affect our health.

In light of these perspectives, the church has an important role to perform.

4. Enhance the church as a community of acceptance.

In light of the ambiguities of the relationship between sin and sickness; Christ's response to illness by healing, not judging; the Gospel mandate to bear one another's burdens, the church's response to persons with AIDS should be to create a community of acceptance, to practice a personal ethic of compassion, and to bring healing wherever possible.

In responding to the AIDS crisis, one of the key tests for the religious community and specifically the Christian church is how seriously they take the church as the body of Christ. This image of the church reflects the view that if one member suffers, we all suffer — it is not *we* vs. *they*, but *us*. As Robert Lambourne expressed it: He only is whole who shares in the brokenness of others. The AIDS crisis should not simply produce anxieties of self-protection but compassion for those with AIDS. Furthermore, with ten or more reported cases of Roman Catholic priests with AIDS, a Methodist bishop dying from AIDS, as well as numerous church members, the church is not immune from this tragedy.

As Bernie Brown, S.J., wrote on an ethic of acceptance for persons with AIDS, the church has been at the vanguard of such a ministry. As Jesus walked among the lepers and the medieval church set up the first hospitals for sick strangers, so we must welcome the person with AIDS as our neighbor, that is, as the person in need. Judgment in the face of sickness simply does not have a place; we cannot care for the lung cancer patient who smoked for 20 years, the liver-damaged alcoholic, or the high-speed car accident driver on the one hand, and on the other hand judge the person with AIDS as not deserving care. This does not mean we ignore the relationship between decisions and consequences in illness but to say, despite the stupidity of the decision, we will care for the patient.

Fortunately, the church is recognizing its responsibility. In Washington, D.C., we have held several church-sponsored conferences on AIDS. The Damien Ministry, started by a priest, is a house for patients with AIDS. Mother Theresa, as well, has established a home for their care. The World Council of Churches Executive Committee in June 1986 held a consultation in Geneva on AIDS and the Church as a Healing Community and recommended three responses for the church: (1) pastoral care; (2) education for prevention; and (3) social ministry.

5. Bearing one another's burdens.

Galatians 6 provides an injunction for our response to persons with AIDS. When Paul writes to the Galatians, he refers to bearing one another's burdens, standing by one another, helping one another. We cannot stand by and say, "Look at that poor person with AIDS, what will become of him?" We have to be with that person, caring for him or her, or we are worse off than the sick person. This verse of bearing one another's burdens is exactly within the context of those who have brought misfortune on themselves.

We are in no position to condemn, but only to help, to respond to others' needs. Bearing one another's burdens involves being with people where they are and, whenever possible, changing the circumstances that put them there in the first place. To bear one another's burdens means to lighten the burden of physical pain, fear of death, ostracization, and loneliness of the person dying of AIDS. Unless we stand with our brother or sister, how can we bear the name of Jesus Christ? However, the patient also must be responsible. The second half of this passage is "carry your own load." We are accountable. We live in a broken world. In this setting, AIDS patients must follow treatment, cultivate a hopeful attitude, and marshall all the resources to combat their illness. Resignation is not the only response.

6. Offer the resources of healing.

The third response of the church to persons with AIDS is to share all the resources of healing. At first blush, these may appear cruel and empty words with the uniformly fatal nature of AIDS. How can we speak of healing in the midst of inevitable and painful death? First, it is important that we are knowledgeable about available medical treatment. This includes care of a palliative nature or experimental drugs such as AZT or measures that treat the secondary infections related to AIDS. The church should assist with funds and referral for patients to receive the best medical and nursing care available.

Second, and most important, the church should have services of prayer and healing not only for AIDS patients but for all in need of healing. Often the family and friends are every bit as much in need of healing as the persons with AIDS. These healing resources should not be viewed as magic rites or spiritual incantations but a receiving of the power of God who is the source of all healing. God is never limited by our perspectives of what conditions can be healed. With God, all things are possible. Hence, the liturgical and devotional resources for healing may provide a sense of hope in the midst of despair. Especially within the Reformed Christian tradition, a rediscovery of the sacraments, including the annointing with oil, is important for the full range of potential healing. However, one word of caution is in order. We need to avoid claiming that strong faith and prayer will automatically bring physical healing. If this is done, the sick person may carry a double burden — the burden of the physical illness and the burden that their faith was inadequate. However, even when physical healing is not possible, spiritual, emotional, and mental healing may take place.

In conclusion, the task of religious educators and other leaders within the church is to replace fear of AIDS by compassion and caring for persons with AIDS and to work for the prevention of some cases of AIDS by promoting healthy sexual lifestyles within a religious perspective of the beauty of love in all its forms.

Dr. Evans is director of new programs and senior staff associate, Kennedy Institute of Ethics, Georgetown University.

BIBLIOGRAPHY

Allen, Virginia E. "AIDS: Facts and Fears." *Midwest Medical Ethics*, Vol. 2, No. 4 (Fall 1986), pp. 3-4.

Altman, Lawrence K. "Health Experts Find No Evidence to Link AIDS to Kissing." *New York Times*, June 8, 1987.

American Red Cross. *Facts About AIDS*. Washington, DC: American Red Cross.

"A Patient's Bill of Rights." *Journal of Humanistic Psychology* 21(3), Summer 1981, pp. 83-84.

Arno, Peter S. "AIDS: A Balancing Act of Resources." *Business and Health*, December 1986, pp. 20-24.

Barron, James. "Koch Orders New AIDS Ad Stressing Sexual Abstinence." *New York Times*, pp. A1 & B7.

Boodman, Sandra G. "Meese Orders AIDS Test for New U.S. Parolees." *Washington Post*, June 9, 1987, p. A4.

Boodman, Sandra G. "Priests and AIDS: Will Church Minister to Its Own?" *Washington Post*, February 7, 1987, pp. A1 and A9.

Boodman, Sandra G., and Okie, Susan. "Aggressive Prevention Efforts Proliferate: WHO Official Calls for World Cooperation, Warning There Are No Geographic 'Safe Areas.' " *Washington Post,* June 5, 1987, p. D1.

Bove, Joseph R. "How Should We Handle the Ethical Questions Regarding Information to Donors and Patients and the Practical Implications Regarding Deferral of Donors and Handling of Donated Blood in the Event of Introducing a Screening Test for HTLV-III as in Order to Prevent Transmission of AIDS by Blood Transfusion." *International Forum,* 49 (1985), pp. 234-239.

Brown, Bernard J. "Creative Acceptance: An Ethics for AIDS." Unpublished Manuscript, 1987.

Brown, Bernard J. "Religious Educating in Sexual Ethics: Towards Compliance or Wisdom?" Unpublished Manuscript, 1987.

Buckley, William F., Jr. ". . . And the Move to Testing." *Washington Post,* June 7, 1987.

Buckley, William F., Jr. "Reservations About Dr. Koop's Advice . . ." *Washington Post,* October 28, 1986.

Caceres, C. A., M.D. "Questions on 'AIDS.' " *Health Street* (Washington, DC: Institute for Technology in Health Care, 1984).

Centers for Disease Control. CDC Protocol #732A, "Epidemiologic Studies of HTLV-III/LAV in Selected Populations of Women." February 13, 1986.

Centers for Disease Control. "Education and Foster Care of Children Infected with Human T-Lymphotropic Virus Type III/Lymphadenopathy-Associated Virus." *Morbidity and Mortality Weekly Report,* Vol. 34, No. 34 (August 30, 1985): 517-521.

Coffin, William Sloane. "AIDS." *Sermons from Riverside* (New York: Riverside Church, January 26, 1986).

Colburn, Don. "AIDS: A National Turning Point." *Washington Post,* June 9, 1987, Health Section, pp. 8-10.

Colburn, Don. "AIDS: The Growing Impact." *Washington Post,* June 2, 1987, Health Section, pp. 10-14.

Cowell, Alan. "AIDS Casts Shadow on a Greek Isle." *New York Times,* May 25, 1987.

Crenshaw, Theresa L., M.D. "AIDS Update: Condoms are Not Enough." *AASECT Newsletter,* Vol. 18 (April 1987), pp. 20, 22.

Culverhouse, Tricia J., M.A. "Tips Toward Inclusiveness: Responding as the Body of Christ to the AIDS Crisis." *Special Edition,* 1986.

"Despite Test, AIDS Virus Transmitted in Transplant." *Washington Post,* May 29, 1987, p. A3.

d'Oronzio, Joseph C. "Coming to Terms." *Critical Choice,* Vol. 1, No. 2 (Spring 1987), p. 2.

Dobbs, Michael. "Syphilis War of '30s Fuels AIDS Debate: Conservatives See Campaign as Model." *Washington Post,* June 7, 1987, pp. A12-A13.

Drotman, D. Peter, M.D. "Now is the Time to Prevent AIDS." *Critical Choice,* Vol. 1, No. 2 (Spring 1987), pp. 1, 4-5.

Flanigan, Rosemary. "AIDS: Duty to the Individual or Duty to Society." *Midwest Medical Ethics,* Vol. 2., No. 4 (Fall 1986), pp. 2, 8.

Gellman, Barton. "Tracing AIDS Cases Raises Privacy Issue." *Washington Post,* July 18, 1983, pp. A1, A4.

Goodman, Ellen. "The AIDS Carrier as Criminal." *Washington Post,* June 9, 1987, p. A21.

Goodman, Ellen. ". . . And the New Fear of Sex." *Washington Post,* October 28, 1986.

Hilts, Philip J. "Method of Testing AIDS Drug Raises Ethical Questions." *Washington Post,* September 14, 1986, pp. A1, A17.

Holy Bible. Revised Standard Version. New York: William Collins Sons & Co., 1952.

Koop, C. Everett. *Surgeon General's Report on Acquired Immune Deficiency Syndrome* (Washington, DC: Department of Health and Human Services, 1986).

Longone, John. "AIDS Update: Still No Reason for Hysteria." *Discover,* September 1986, pp. 28-47.

Lewis, C. S. *The Four Loves* (New York: Harcourt Brace Jovanovich, 1960).

Louria, Donald B., M.D. "Exclusive Interview: The Social Impact of Panic Over AIDS." *Critical Choice,* Vol. I., No. 2 (Spring 1987), pp. 3-7.

Mass, Lawrence, M.D. *Medical Answers About AIDS* (New York: Gay Men's Health Crisis, 1985).

May, William. *Passionate Attachments: Thinking About Love* (New York: Free Press, in press).

McCarthy, Colman. "AIDS: Waves of Panic." *Washington Post*, June 13, 1987, p. A23.

McGilvray, J. C., ed. *The Quest for Health: An Interim Report of a Study Process* (Cleator Moor, England: Bethwaites Printers, 1979).

"Netherlands — AIDS euthanasia mecca?" *American Medical News*, May 22, 1987.

Pear, Robert. "AIDS Feared as Occupational Hazard." *New York Times*, May 24, 1987.

Randolph, Eleanor. "AIDS Reporters' Challenge: To Educate, Not Panic, the Public." *Washington Post*, June 5, 1987, p. D1.

"Relationship of the Christian Faith to Health." Report of the 172nd General Assembly of the United Presbyterian Church of the United States of America (Philadelphia: Office of the General Assembly, 1960).

"Revelation of AIDS Death was Resisted." *Boston Globe*, May 26, 1987.

Rovner, Sandy. "The Epidemic Course: Women and Children Last?" *Washington Post*, June 9, 1987, Health Section, pp. 8-9.

Scanzoni, Lisa. *Is the Homosexual my Neighbor?* (New York: Harper & Row, 1980).

Sendzik, Dan. "The Church & AIDS: Reality & Response." *AIDS: A Resource Packet for Congregations*. New York: AIDS Task Force, National Council of Churches of Christ, 1986.

"Should AIDS testing be a requirement to obtain insurance?" *Midwest Medical Ethics*, Vol. 2, No. 4 (Fall 1986), pp. 4-6.

Strong, James. *Strong's Exhaustive Concordance* (Michigan: Associated Publishers, n.d.).

"Survey Finds Support for AIDS Patients." *New York Times*, May 22, 1987.

Tate, Wendy. "Facing the AIDS Epidemic: Will Fear or Faith Prevail?" *Engage/Social Action* (February 1986).

Thompson, Larry. "AIDS Therapies Showing Promise: Measures Range from Early Detection to Boosting Immune System." *Washington Post*, June 7, 1987, pp. A4-A5.

Victorian AIDS Council. "Prevention Education Strategy." 1985.

Westburg, Granger. *Theological Roots of Wholistic Health Care* (Hinsdale, IL: Wholistic Health Centers, Inc., 1979).

Will, George F. "AIDS: The Real Danger." *Washington Post*, June 7, 1987.

Wing, David L. "AIDS and Handicap Discrimination Laws." *Midwest Medical Ethics*, Vol. 2, No. 4 (Fall 1986), pp. 1, 6.

THE CHALLENGE TO THE CHRISTIAN COMMUNITY

Michael F. Duffy

James Madison University
Harrisonburg, Virginia

I

The presence and spread of AIDS pose moral challenges at every level of society. Individuals, many of whom are accustomed to a climate of relative freedom in sexual behavior, must rethink the meaning of sexual responsibility. Health care professionals face such questions as whether they will perform surgery on those who test positive for the HIV antibody. Businesses are called upon to devise and implement nondiscriminatory policies regarding workers who are antibody positive or who develop symptoms of ARC or full-blown AIDS. Society in all its sectors is called upon to evidence compassion and justice in the face of widespread suffering and fear. Although this essay will focus on the responsibilities facing one particular sector, namely the Christian community, the methodology recommended and many of the conclusions drawn are certainly meaningful beyond that scope.

There are several methods by which one may address moral problems and issues. One may, for example, derive moral principles from hypothetical social contracts, or discern moral responsibilities through an analysis of the experience of moral requiredness, or recommend those actions that result in the maximization of certain values and the minimization of others.[1] Differing expressions of a further approach, one which views community as

---

[1] For examples, see respectively John Rawls, *A Theory of Justice* (Cambridge, MA: Harvard University Press, 1971); Arthur Dyck, "Moral Requiredness: Bridging the Gap Between 'Ought' and 'Is' — part 1," in *The Journal of Religious Ethics*, volume 6:2, Fall, 1978, pp. 293-318; Joseph Fletcher, *Situation Ethics* (Philadelphia: The Westminster Press, 1966). Fletcher's position has changed significantly since this work, but is still clearly consequentialist.

the focus of moral discernment and moral life, can be found in the work of such thinkers as Martin Buber and Stanley Hauerwas. Although it is not possible here fully to assess this method in any of its forms, or to contrast it with the other possibilities, much of its appeal lies in its assumption that community is one essential aspect of human flourishing and in its emphasis upon the relationships between people rather than on the "rights" or "autonomy" of individuals.[2]

A formalized version of a community-centered method will be developed in this essay. It is my contention that moral responsibilities may be discerned through an analysis of the concept of community and then fulfilled through the attempt to foster what prove to be essential community-making and community-sustaining features. The analysis of the nature of *Christian* community, of course, may vary from the analysis of community in general, both in the understanding of and in the importance attributed to certain of the highlighted features.

There are two central elements in the concept of community. The first is that there is a common purpose or common center around which people are gathered. H. Tristram Engelhardt in his recent *The Foundations of Bioethics* defines community as "a voluntary association of individuals through a common concrete view of the good."[3] That is, people who agree on the end or ends of life, or on what is morally permissable or required action and what is not, may join together voluntarily to pursue common goals. Although Hauerwas's views differ from those of Engelhardt in several crucial respects, his characterization of community has a similar focus. In his *Community of Character*, Hauerwas says, "a community is a group of persons who share a history and whose common set of interpretations about that history provide the basis for common actions."[4] The model he has in mind, of course, is the Christian community, whose members may be led to worship, act nonviolently, etc., through their common understandings of the gospel message. A third characterization, which highlights this first feature, is the vision of community presented by Martin Buber in his *I and Thou*:

---

[2] Within a specifically Christian context, the concept of community gets its strength from the numerous New Testament passages which focus upon what it means to be a community of Christians. Examples include Philippians 2, Acts 4:32-37, Romans 12, etc.

[3] H. Tristram Engelhardt, *The Foundations of Bioethics* (New York: Oxford University Press, 1986), p. 49.

[4] Stanley Hauerwas, *A Community of Character* (Notre Dame: University of Notre Dame Press, 1981), p. 60.

. . . [the relations of persons] with their true *Thou*, the radial lines that proceed from all the points of the *I* to the Center, form a circle. It is not the periphery, the community, that comes first, but the radii, the common quality of relation with the Center. This alone guarantees the authentic existence of the community.[5]

Buber's image of the circle is appropriate. The radii indicate the relationship that must exist between each member of the community and the common center or purpose, a relationship without which the community ceases to be a community. The nature of this relationship is perhaps best seen as one of commitment. If some in an actual community lose their initial commitment to the common purpose, the community will, under most circumstances, begin to fragment.

There is an exception to this consequence, and it highlights the second feature of community. Even if persons lose their commitment to the common center around which they were gathered, the community may still thrive if they retain their commitment to one another. Under these conditions, the original purpose may become modified or reinterpreted in order to accommodate the changing commitments or perspectives of certain of the members. Whatever the mechanics of this process, it indicates that the other central feature of community lies in the common bonds shared by its members. Buber's image of the circle is again appropriate, as the arcs that connect the persons along the periphery may be taken to represent the bonds or commitments between them.

Any living community, insofar as it is a community, will evidence these two general features. Its members will to some degree be committed to one another and to a common purpose or center. And insofar as community is sought as an end, perhaps because of its general value for human flourishing or because of the models offered by early Christianity, there are two ways in which it may be pursued — attaining agreement on ends or promoting and nourishing the sorts of bonds between people that are necessary for community to be a reality. Given our widely pluralistic culture and world, the strengthening of our communities and the expanding of their boundaries[6] are less likely to come about

---

[5] Martin Buber, *I and Thou* (New York: Charles Scribner's Sons, 1958), translated by Ronald Gregor Smith, p. 115.

[6] Of course, not all living communities are morally worthy of being expanded and strengthened. Judgments on this issue will be made by way of moral evaluation of the center around which the community is gathered. This process entails issues well beyond the scope of this paper.

through finding a common end on which all agree than it is through the fostering of the relevant commitment between people.

One crucial aspect of this commitment, that is, one of the foundational bonds that makes a community a community, lies in the willingness of persons to be present to one another in times of suffering and need. Presence is essentially a matter of availability to and caring for the other; its opposite is captured in the concepts of indifference, abandonment, and desertion. When persons are suffering or in need, and are left to their own resources, the community necessarily fragments. On the model of the parable of the Good Samaritan, to leave by the wayside those who need help and caring is to endanger the foundation of commitment to one another by which any community survives. The attempt to stand beside the other rather than walking away from or ignoring the other is crucial to community life, and especially to the life of the Christian community. To put it in Hauerwas's words, "For what does God require of us other than our unfailing presence in the midst of the world's suffering and pain?"[7]

This theme of presence instructs the Christian community of its responsibilities in the face of the AIDS challenge. And these responsibilities are not only focused upon those who are suffering and are within a particular parish, or upon those who consider themselves to be Christian, but must also be directed toward the world as a whole, for which the Christian community seeks to make God's love a reality. This is perhaps most clearly seen through noting the strong connection between the understanding of presence at work here and the basic Christian norm of *agape*. Caring presence is, perhaps, a common thread that runs through most understandings of *agape*, whether stated in terms of equal regard, self-sacrifice, or friendship and mutuality.[8] Despite their differing theoretical roots and practical implications, each includes the expressing of God's continuing presence. The com-

---

[7] Stanley Hauerwas, *Suffering Presence* (Notre Dame: University of Notre Dame Press, 1986), p. 80. The reader will note that I have been greatly influenced by Hauerwas and especially by this work. Thus there are similarities between Hauerwas's emphasis upon presence and my own. I am more interested, however, in a systematic derivation and application of the concept.

[8] The classic analysis and consideration of the different interpretations of *agape* is, of course, Gene Outka's *Agape: An Ethical Analysis* (New Haven: Yale University Press, 1972). For an emphasis on Christian love as mutuality, see Margaret Farley's "New Patterns of Relationship: Beginnings of a Moral Revolution," in Walter Burkhardt, ed., *Woman: New Dimensions* (New York: Paulist Press, 1975), pp. 51-70.

mitment to be a caring presence calls forth response to the AIDS crisis at several levels.

The most basic and obvious relevant responsibilities of the community that is Christian are focused on the direct presence provided by personal contact and on the less direct presence of policies and programs that seek to address the needs of those directly affected by AIDS or by related illness. At the most personal level, although counseling and medical attention are important, presence may best be expressed through listening, sitting together in silence, or a caring touch. It is this sort of presence that is so often being withheld from persons with AIDS. As stated in a Report of the Council for Health and Human Services Ministries of the United Church of Christ, "[r]epeatedly, persons who have AIDS tell counselors or caregivers that they have not been touched by another person other than for clinical reasons since their diagnosis."[9] To counter this isolating trend, persons who belong to communities seeking to be Christian must reach out. Asked what personal ministry to those with AIDS entails, one person responded, "A hug once in a while would be nice."[10] A caring hug is perhaps the most basic form of presence possible between two people.

Christian communities must also advocate programs and policies that combat the societal-level abandonment often experienced by those with AIDS. Insurance companies, businesses, health care professionals, town and city governments, school systems, landlords — all of these should be encouraged to consider and address the concerns of persons with AIDS in ways that simultaneously recognize their suffering, the lack of danger they pose to those around them, and the fact that they are often still quite able to be contributing members to society. The presence called for by the moral decision-making method can either manifest itself in or be entirely absent from the encounters between those who make and enact policies and those in need. The method provides the discernment that only the manifestation, and not the absence, is moral.

---

[9] "The Church and AIDS," *The Council for Health and Human Service Ministries Report*, Volume 4, Spring 1987, p. 28.

[10] Andrés Tapia, "How Churches Can Get Involved," *Christianity Today*, August 7, 1987, p. 18.

II

These two basic types of presence have education as their pre-requisite. Education is the necessary condition for enabling and motivating people to respond in the ways discussed here and is thus itself another moral responsibility. It is also a still further form of caring presence, both to those who are fearful about the disease or about the other issues connected with it, such as sexuality and death, and to those at risk of acquiring the disease. There are at least two crucial elements to any education program about AIDS, both of which should be taken up by the churches. The first is sex education.

Central to debates over the teaching of sex education has been the concern over whether teaching about contraception contributes to participation in sexual activities. Those who have held that it does contribute have gone on to argue against such teaching either because of opposition to certain sexual activities in and of themselves or because of interest in preventing teenage pregnancies and/or the spread of sexually transmitted diseases. The degree of harm caused by the HIV, in conjunction with the fact that the estimated 1.5 million persons exposed to the virus can transmit it (even though they evidence no symptoms), transforms this discussion. The same realities that give additional support to calls for abstinence also lend support to the call for explicit teaching about sexual activities and contraception.

On the one hand, no sexual (or other) behaviors that put someone at risk of receiving the virus can express the concern for one another that is necessary for any community that calls itself moral. Thus, there are only two possible ways to be sexually responsible in the current climate: either one must know his or her antibody status and act accordingly, or one must act as if one is antibody positive and can transmit the HIV. That is, one must abstain from all risky behavior unless one knows that one's antibody status is negative. To have such knowledge, one must either have received a confirmed negative test result[11] or never have engaged in any risky activity and never have been exposed to the virus through a blood transfusion, needle-stick injury, or related incident.

On the other hand, it is wise to recognize that persons growing

---

[11] Under what conditions, if any, one has a moral responsibility to be tested, as opposed to abstaining from all risky behavior, is a problem I have addressed in an unpublished paper, tentatively entitled "Privacy, Trust, and Community." Confidentiality will be a major factor, given the discrimination and violence which is being directed at persons with AIDS.

up in the last two or three decades, and thus accustomed to a fairly free sexual environment, are unlikely to eliminate all sexual expression from their behavior. People are simply going to participate in various sexual activities. Under these circumstances, anything other than explicit presentation of the ways in which the risk of transmission can be reduced or eliminated, without the elimination of all sexual contact, would seem to be a form of desertion. It is preferable to educate people as to what are and what are not safe sexual activities than not to teach this care and perhaps silently cooperate in the spread of the HIV.[12]

Such education is appropriate within and by the church that seeks to make the caring presence of God a reality in others' lives. It is a necessary condition of preventing the spread of the disease. It precedes and eliminates the need for immediate presence in suffering by reducing the numbers of persons affected by AIDS and is to be encouraged. Not to educate, and thus to support the lack of information and the misinformation that abounds in all sectors and age-groups in society, is essentially to abandon people to increased risk of harm and to the fear lack of knowledge often brings. It is to be moralistic rather than moral.

The second manifestation of educational presence beyond direct sex education lies in teaching people how to be present to those who need their care, be it physical, emotional, or spiritual. Again, teaching the facts with respect to the spread of the HIV is a prerequisite, as it provides people with the recognition that these sorts of presence are not harmful to them. As time moves on and most of our churches find they have members who have ARC or AIDS or are related to or concerned with people suffering in this way, they will need to know how to meet the challenge of overcoming their fears and anxieties. To address these fears and anxieties and move one another to the place where they can be overcome is to express community-sustaining care for one another. The alternative is to allow people to ignore the need, to remain safe from the suffering but also "safe" from the challenge of God that we be present to those in need.

Each of the responsibilities presented above may equally well apply to the non-Christian community as to the Christian, even

---

[12] Risky activities include unprotected intercourse, sharing IV drug needles, oral sex on a male without a condom and oral sex on a woman, and masturbation on broken skin. Safe activities include dry kissing, masturbation on healthy skin, and fantasy. Protected intercourse is certainly safer than unprotected intercourse, though it is not absolutely without risk.

though the argument has generally been made with respect to the latter. Personal contact, advocacy, and education in its various forms are all aspects or types of caring presence and, as such, are universal moral responsibilities on the community method articulated in this paper. There is, however, another challenge that presents itself more specifically to the Christian community than to community in general. It reflects such events in the Christian tradition as the command of Jesus to take up the cross and follow him, the actions of Jesus in eating with those who were despised, and so on. It finds theoretical focus in one understanding of the relation between God's role and the role of human beings in history.

There are two basic views one may take on the nature of this relation, although actual positions will often be a blending of the two types. One corresponds roughly to consequentialist models of moral decision-making. This is a major aspect of the theology of the Social Gospel and of certain liberation theologies today and emphasizes the human role in the structures and outcomes of history. On this view, the mission of the church is generally seen as being focused on effecting change in the world. The above discussions of advocacy and education exemplify this type.

On the other hand, to emphasize *God's* role in and control of the outcome of history is to locate one's responsibilities in expressing certain values rather than achieving certain ends. This approach corresponds roughly to the deontological emphasis in ethical theory and may be seen in the writings of people such as Stanley Hauerwas and John Howard Yoder. Although it would be a mistake to see no concern within this view for the consequences of action, its focus is not on influencing people or institutions but on living truthfully. The community that seeks to be Christian and to express God's presence will understand its responsibilities to extend beyond those discussed above.

Those who seek to be Christian may find their unique responsibility in the notion of identification, perhaps the deepest expression of presence. To witness to the presence of God's love is not only not to abandon those in need, but it is to put oneself on the line in order to witness to that presence to a world that succumbs to the temptation of abandonment. To reach out to those who suffer and to confront the world on their behalf from a position of power is one thing; to become powerless as they are powerless is quite another and entails different behavior on the part of the Christian community.

In a colloquium in which I participated, one person asked why it was we could not just quarantine everyone with AIDS. One hopes, and we should all work to ensure, that society does not give in to this temptation of desertion, especially given the fact that AIDS is spread only in specific ways. However, should the barbaric happen, the community that seeks to identify itself with those who are thus outcast ought to go into quarantine with them. This would be the deepest expression of presence and witness. It would witness to "God's unfailing presence," to repeat Hauerwas's words, demonstrating this presence to the outcast group and to those doing the casting out. It could still be done in the hope of fostering the bonds of community but would testify to the direction in which the presence of the Christian community must turn if society fractures to such an extent that the hope for the spread of community through the fostering of bonds of presence between people is drastically reduced.

Another similar, though less drastic, example is found in a proposal made in reaction to the recent call to test all hospital patients for the antibodies to the AIDS virus. The proposal is that all health care professionals be tested first. To do this is to take the chance of being as vulnerable as the patient, to take the chance of being stigmatized by the results of a positive test becoming known, and thus it is to identify with patients in a certain way. It is to create or sustain bonds of community, at least within the hospital setting but with implications beyond that setting, by risking the presence of identification.

On such a model, a further way of witness for the members of the Christian community might be voluntarily to be tested, to be public about the fact that one is being tested, but not to reveal the test results to any who do not need to know. Certainly, if one is considering sexual relations with another person, then that person must be informed of one's status. But unless there are such concerns at hand, not to reveal the results allows one the opportunity to educate others in a powerful way, challenging them to think about their fear, and to consider whether they will be present with and hug someone who may be antibody-positive. It thus enables one to be a caring presence to those who are stigmatized by what others suspect (with or without foundation) in regard to their capacity to spread AIDS, as well as to those who accept the challenge to understand the point one is trying to make in identifying oneself with those stigmatized.

There are many other ways to express and foster presence to

one another in the face of the serious moral challenges of AIDS. To enter the swimming pool where the person with AIDS has been swimming and which everyone else refuses to enter[13] is to be present to the ostracized persons and to seek to be present to those who are fearful. Even if the educational attempt fails, it is to witness to the value of presence that sustains the moral community and to challenge others to be morally responsible in the face of temptation. Likewise, presence for the Christian community means never turning anyone away from participation in the life of a church because they have ARC, AIDS, or because they are in some way identified with the groups whom the virus has hit with the greatest devastation. And, as a final point, it means refusing to go where any of these people find themselves not welcome and perhaps going where they *do* find themselves welcome.

AIDS is frightening. Tens of thousands of people have already died as the result of the virus, and more will die in the future. And the number of deaths does not complete the story of the human suffering connected to the presence and spread of the virus. The options for positive involvement by the Christian community are numerous. The conviction expressed in this paper is that a proper understanding of the value and the nature of community in general, and Christian community in particular, enables discernment of our moral responsibilities and that these responsibilities are at least partly captured in the notion of caring presence. To be present to one another in these is to counter the temptations that lead to fragmentation and to be involved in processes of healing. Only such involvement can be considered moral.

Michael F. Duffy is an instructor in the Department of Philosophy and Religion, James Madison University, and pastor of Bethlehem United Church of Christ, Tenth Legion, Virginia.

---

[13] As one pastor recently did, although I cannot remember who or where.

SAFE SEX AND LOST LOVE

Karen Lebacqz and Deborah Blake

Pacific School of Religion
Berkeley, California

AIDS, "Intercourse," and Sexual Ethics

It is probably no mistake that we use the term "intercourse" to refer both to conversation and to one of the most intimate of sexual acts. How we talk and how we conduct ourselves sexually both say a great deal about us.[1] In this essay, our concern is how the conversation about AIDS in our society affects the possibilities of a Christian sexual ethic. How is the AIDS crisis influencing and directing our discourse about sex and sexuality? What impact does our understanding of AIDS have on sexual ethics?

"Safe sex" has become the contemporary catchword. Advertisements urge it, pamphlets tell us how to practice it, and safe sex clubs have emerged in sections of large cities.[2] But what is "safe sex?" And what is the talk about safe sex doing to the way we think about our sexuality and our community?

The participants needed for this discourse are many. We speak here as Christian ethicists, one Protestant and one Roman Catholic. We believe that there is an important place for the concern about safe sex, but we also contend that the concept may endanger a genuinely Christian sexual ethic. Indeed, we hold that lines delineating proper roles in the discourse have become blurred, with the result that Christians may mistakenly adopt a safe sex standard as adequate for Christian sexual ethics. We will argue that safe sex is a legitimate public health concern but that it is not the same as a Christian sexual ethic.

---

[1] Indeed, in *The Sexual Language* (Ottawa: The U. of Ottawa Press, 1977), Andre Guindon proposes that sexuality is best understood as a form of communication.

[2] Armistead Maupin, well-known author of *Tales of the City* about gay life in San Francisco, interviewed in *The Berkeley Monthly*, September 1987.

Religious Education   Vol 83   No 2   Spring 1988

Public Health Discourse: "Safe Sex"

The role of public health officials is to maintain the health of the community through surveillance, research, prevention, and treatment of disease. In the case of AIDS, initial surveillance and research identified and characterized the disease. The human immunodeficiency virus (HIV) was found to be the causative agent. Patterns of transmission have been identified: The virus is transmitted by entry into one's bloodstream of bodily fluids — specifically blood and semen — which have a transmissible concentration of HIV. People at risk are intravenous drug users sharing needles; fetuses of infected mothers; recipients of contaminated blood products (e.g. hemophiliacs); and those practicing anal intercourse, vaginal intercourse, and possibly oral/genital intercourse with an infected partner.

Direct treatment of AIDS and ARC have been unavailable to date. Since AIDS is a deadly disease, this leaves prevention as the remaining — and urgent — public health action. Screening of blood supplies, avoidance of contaminated needles, and avoidance of high risk genital activity are the major public health strategies to prevent spread of the disease. In particular, "safe sex" education and changes in sexual behavior have been found to be a significant means for reducing the risk of transmission of the AIDS virus.

Thus, "safe sex" has captured the mind of the American public. Safe sex has a decided role to play in protecting the public health by preventing the spread of the disease in populations at risk. It is a worthy and important step in the protection of people's health and lives.

But safe sex, which was intended as a public health measure to prevent disease transmission, has crossed over into the realm of sexual ethics. And it is a sexual ethics characterized by the elements that held Christian sexual ethics in bondage for centuries. We suggest that a proper public health concern for self-protection in the face of the AIDS crisis has become an improper total response to sex and sexuality. There is a place for "safe sex," but only a place. "Safe sex" does not provide an adequate Christian sexual ethic.

Public Discourse: Fear, Physicality, and Blame

The flip side of concern for safety is fear. The undercurrent of the public health discourse that has captured the American imagination is one of defensiveness, self-preservation, and fear. The "sex-can-kill-you" message of the safe sex campaign places an aura of evil around sex and sexuality. It also begins to return our attention solely to the physical: Sex becomes a matter of what "acts" one does and whether the physical parts of our bodies are sufficiently protected (e.g., whether condoms are used). Thus, in the wake of the safe sex campaign, there is a danger that we will return to an earlier era of thinking of sex as basically evil and dangerous and of focusing exclusively on the physical dimensions of it.

Our past tradition of teaching about sexual ethics was built upon a similar basis of fear and focused on the physical act and its consequences. Joseph Fletcher characterized this ethic in a delightful limerick:

> There was a young lady named Wilde
> Who kept herself quite undefiled
> by thinking of Jesus
> and social diseases
> And the fear of having a child.[3]

This is the "safe sex" of a previous age. It was a sexual ethics based on fear. Sex was "defiling," and the way to remain pure was to avoid sexual contact by keeping alive the fears attached to it — fear of pregnancy and fear of sexually transmitted disease.

The safe sex of the present age is not so different. Fear of pregnancy, syphillis, and gonnorhea is replaced by fear of AIDS, but the dominance of fear remains the same. Thus, the contemporary parallel to Fletcher's clever limerick might look like this:

> If safe sex is what you would find,
> To the danger of AIDS don't be blind;
> use condoms with care,
> stay in just one pair,
> Monogamy is not a bind!

"Safe sex" can be variously interpreted to include the use of condoms and non-intrusive sexual play or to mean monogamous long-term sex with a "clean" partner. As Alice Kahn parodies, sex is in danger of becoming so "safe" that we'll never want it again.[4]

Some are glad for the "safe sex" age, feeling that it will reaf-

---

[3] Joseph Fletcher, *Moral Responsibility: Situation Ethics at Work* (Westminster, 1967), p. 88.

[4] Alice Kahn, "Sex So Safe You'll Never Want It Again," *San Francisco Examiner*, Sunday Punch section, August 23, 1987, p. 5.

firm some traditional values of family, monogamy, and careful-
ness with one's body. One gay spokesperson declares, "Now that
the sex has been taken away, the freewheeling sex, I'm left with
the family and it's not so bad to exist with that."[5] In the wake of
fear, some traditional values may reemerge. But fear is not an
acceptable justification for these values.

Fear brings with it an uglier side. Fear and blame are often
companions. So it is in the case of AIDS. A recent survey showed
that while people in the U.S. claim to feel a great deal of compassion for AIDS sufferers (78 percent), less than half (48 percent)
thought that AIDS victims should be allowed to live normally in
the community. Most significantly, nearly half (45 percent)
thought that most people with AIDS have only themselves to
blame, and 42 percent thought that the disease was a punishment
for a decline in moral standards.[6] These poll results coincide with
reports of a suspicious fire that gutted the house of a Florida family whose three sons, all hemophiliacs, are infected with the HIV
virus, though they do not yet exhibit signs of AIDS. The advent of
AIDS has sparked public hysteria and fear-based responses to
sexuality.[7]

Moreover, in the mind of the American public, it would seem,
AIDS is linked inextricably to the gay community.[8] AIDS is a serious problem among intravenous drug users, but it is the transmission of AIDS through sexual contact — particularly homosexual contact — that has captured the American imagination. The
fact that AIDS is *not* a "gay" phenomenon elsewhere in the world
has had seemingly little impact on the American perception.

This linking of AIDS and gay sexuality in the popular mind is
important. It affects and even determines the way we respond to
the AIDS epidemic. Because we have seen AIDS as a "gay" issue,

---

[5] Maupin, *The Berkeley Monthly*, p. 19.

[6] George Gallup, Jr., "ID Cards Favored for AIDS Sufferers," San Francisco Chronicle, vol. 123, no. 194, August 31, 1987, p. 7.

[7] James Nelson notes that fear is the dynamic underlying the vindictive and punitive
attitudes of the religious right. The fear is fed by a pervasive dualism that has both political
and sexual manifestations: politically, it divides the world into "good" capitalists and
"bad" communists; sexually, it divides the sexes into a hierarchical ordering and divides
the "good" soul from the "bad" body. In short, the world can be divided into "good" and
"bad" people, those who are "saved" and those who are "damned." Among the "damned"
are all those who do not fit the traditional, narrowly-drawn sex role stereotypes and sexual
behavior patterns. *Between Two Gardens* (NY: Pilgrim Press, 1983), chapter 9.

[8] Dennis Altman, *AIDS in the Mind of America: The Social, Political, and Psychological Impact of a New Epidemic* (Garden City, N.Y.: Doubleday, 1986).

we have seen it as a gay problem and responsibility rather than as a health problem and public responsibility. Our health resources have been slow to respond.[9] Families of victims have been afraid to seek assistance for fear of stigmatization.[10] Harrassment of gay men has increased since public awareness of AIDS.[11] Curt Clinkscales, head of the National Alliance of Senior Citizens and a self-characterized conservative Republican and Reagan supporter, nonetheless criticizes Reagan's newly-appointed panel on AIDS for trying to turn AIDS into an issue of homosexual lifestyle: "All the Commission will be is a sounding board for people who look at AIDS as a curse of God."[12]

In short, along with fear of AIDS and the campaign for "safe sex" comes blame: blame of the victims of AIDS for their own plight and blame of the gay community for promulgating a disease on society. AIDS is the "price" anyone pays for being sexually active, and those who have sex with their own kind are accused of deliberately putting everyone at risk.

Thus, we might add a second verse to our contemporary limerick:

> There was a young man named Rex
> Who with his own kind enjoyed sex.
> The price that he paid
> was that he got AIDS,
> Thus "proving" that he was a hex.

When sex is discussed under the rubric of safety, the gay community is blamed for making the rest of the world not "safe," and the individual AIDS patient is blamed for not having practiced safe sex. "God 'AIDS' the gays" reads one church sign.[13] American sympathies may go out to those who contracted AIDS through blood transfusions or other "faultless" means but not to those whose disease is considered the result of — indeed, the divine

---

[9] For a discussion, see Altman, *AIDS in the Mind of America*, pp. 40-57.

[10] See Earl E. Shelp, Ronald H. Sunderland, and Peter W. A. Mansell, eds., *AIDS: Personal Stories in Pastoral Perspective* (N.Y.: Pilgrim, 1986), p. 108: "With few exceptions these families had decided to withhold information from pastors and congregations. . . . They did not wish to expose themselves and their families to the stigma that they were painfully aware most people applied to the illness and its victims."

[11] Craig Wilson, "Gay Harrassment is Increasing," *USA Today*, July 14, 1987, p. 10.

[12] Quoted by Elizabeth Fernandez in *The San Francisco Examiner*, Sunday August 23, 1987, p. 1. Fernandez charges that the panel "is largely composed of conservatives who conform to an ideology espoused by the Reagan administration but rejected by mainstream medical authorities."

[13] Shelp et. al., *AIDS: Personal Stories*, p. 107.

punishment for — their "lifestyle." "Fear of the disease has become a facade for the expression of latent hatred for and oppression of homosexual people."[14]

We may not have totally reverted to the days when sex was "defiling," but we are not far from thinking that sex is dirty or wrong because it is so inextricably linked to disease and death. Safe sex may be important as a public health measure, but it has brought with it a public discourse in which fear dominates, coupled with a return to physicality in the sexual arena. Fear fosters a rise of blaming responses in the social arena.

The Discourse of Christian Sexual Ethics

Our past tradition of teaching about sexual ethics was built upon a similar basis of fear and focused on the physical while also denigrating the body. Sexuality was understood to be basically evil. This ethics grew out of and was sustained by the Gnostic, Greek, Jansennist, and Puritan influence on the developing church.

In recent years, however, there has been a significant development in Christian approaches to sexual ethics.[15] Working from Scripture, church tradition, the empirical sciences, philosophy, and the experience of church communities, a changed view of sexuality has emerged.

This view sees human sexuality in broad terms: "Human sexuality . . . is our way of being in the world as female or male persons."[16] It is profoundly good. It involves the person at all levels of existence — personal and social, psychological, biological, and spiritual:

> The mystery of sexuality is the mystery of the human need to reach out for the physical and spiritual embrace of others. Sexuality thus expressed God's intention that people find authentic humanness not in isolation but in relationship. In sum, sexuality involves more than what we do with our genitals. More fundamentally, it is who we are as body-

---

[14] Shelp et. al., *AIDS: Personal Stories*, p. 75.

[15] A helpful overview is provided in James P. Hanigan, *What Are They Saying About Sexual Morality?* (N.Y.: Paulist Press, 1982). See also Lisa Sowle Cahill, *Between the Sexes: Foundations for a Christian Ethics of Sexuality* (Philadelphia: Fortress, 1985); Philip S. Keane, *Sexual Morality: A Catholic Perspective* (N.Y.: Paulist, 1977); James B. Nelson, *Embodiment: An Approach to Sexuality and Christian Theology* (Minneapolis: Augsburg, 1978); Anthony Kosnik et. al., *Human Sexuality: New Directions in Catholic Moral Thought* (N.Y.: Paulist, 1977); The United Church of Christ, *Human Sexuality: A Preliminary Study* (N.Y.: United Church Pess, 1977).

[16] James Nelson, *Between Two Gardens*, p. 5.

selves who experience the emotional, cognitive, physical, and spiritual need for intimate communion, both creaturely and divine.[17]

In short, human sexuality in contemporary Christian ethics is seen as primarily relational, spiritual, and integral to our very humanness.

A Christian sexual ethic, then, is not confined to concerns for "safe sex," nor is it a code of sexual behavior.[18] It is built upon an anthropology of human wholeness and affirms the goodness of sexuality and its essential relationality.

Discourse in the Gay Community

It is the gay community that has been most profoundly devastated by the AIDS epidemic in America. And it is this community that reveals some of the most helpful insights about the meaning of sexuality in the face of a deadly epidemic. Frankness in the discussion of "safe sex" is bringing discourse about sex and sexuality out of its shroud of secrecy. As those who have AIDS speak of their disease and of their lives, the closet of homosexuality is being opened, the secrecy and myths are being dispelled.

"Bob," for example, entered gay life after a divorce, having never had a relationship with a man before. "He is a man of moderation, integrity, goals, and ability."[19] After learning that he had ARC, Bob stopped being genitally active. Bob reflects on his sexuality in language reminiscent of that used by Christian ethicist James Nelson: " 'Homosexuality . . . is not what one does sexually. It is an emotional desire. It's still love.' " Bob argues that " 'everything that can exist in heterosexual relationships can exist in homosexual relationships' " and concludes that " 'if God approves of one, then God must approve of the other.' "[20]

At the other end of the spectrum is "Alan." Alan went through two profound changes in his sexual life. Originally, he thought of sexual intercourse as a "special, consummate act." But when he

---

[17] James Nelson, *Between Two Gardens*, p. 6.

[18] This essay is written in response to a position statement that asks, "Is it possible to develop, within a religious framework, a sexual moral code which will protect individuals from sexually transmitted disease and, possibly, death?" We take exception to this framing of the question. To begin with the assumption that we should develop a *protective* sexual ethic is already to presume the very question that should be under consideration: What are the grounds for a *Christian* sexual ethic?

[19] Shelp et. al., *AIDS: Personal Stories*, p. 56.

[20] Ibid., p. 59.

first entered gay life "he had no role models." He therefore went to bars seven nights a week, thinking that this was what gay men did. Sex was reinterpreted for him in the gay bar scene, where he participated in "fast and easy sex."[21] Then, when he was diagnosed with ARC in 1983, he changed his lifestyle again.

"In retrospect," claim the editors of this volume, "Alan regrets that his self-esteem was so low that he felt his only avenue of affirmation was in settings conducive to dangerous conduct."[22] In short, Alan participated in fast and easy sex because it was his way of being affirmed as a gay man in the face of the "double life" that he was forced to live, pretending to be heterosexual for the benefit of his family and peers. "If his home and social environment had been more acceptant of homosexuality, perhaps . . . what he and others risked would not have been necessary."[23]

What Have We Learned?

From Christian ethics and from the gay community several lessons may be learned for the development of a Christian sexual ethic in the face of AIDS.

First, an accurate view of the gay community is necessary. Not all gay sex is "fast and easy." Indeed, of the stories of gay men told in *AIDS: Personal Stories in Pastoral Perspective*, almost none fit the stereotype of gay sex as "fast lane" living. Many are stories of long-term, deep, abiding love.

Second, the AIDS crisis should reaffirm our need to reconceptualize sexuality. Armistead Maupin suggests that because some direct modes of sexual contact are not available to those trying to be safe in the AIDS era, sexuality is being re-eroticized and re-romanticized, and the fullness of sexuality is being recaptured.[24] Sexuality is not just what we do with our genitals: it is love and commitment and desire and a total way of being. Christian sexual ethics should be based on a perception of the fullness of sexuality in human life and of its deep connection to intimacy and communion.

Third, many gay men seek loving, committed, careful ways of being sexual in the world. When those ways are denied by the

---

[21] Ibid., p. 62.

[22] Ibid., p. 63.

[23] Ibid.

[24] Armistead Maupin, interviewed in *The Berkeley Monthly.*

larger society, these men may find alternative expressions of sexuality. The discrimination and prejudice gay men encounter can make them retreat to a separate world of baths, bars, and casual sex: "Our society makes us hide this important part of ourselves and denies us access to more conventional ego strokes. So we take to the sheets."[25] Those who would condemn a presumed gay "lifestyle" must ask what they have done to contribute to it.

Fourth, in the face of ARC and AIDS, the gay community has responded well to the cry for "safe sex." Individuals have been very careful to avoid infecting others, and group practices such as "safe sex" clubs have arisen.

But is safe sex necessarily moral sex? Morality and safety are not the same. At the root of moral sex is love and concern for the partner, mutuality and vulnerability, truthfulness, and trust. Sex can be "safe" without exhibiting any of these characteristics.[26] Sex can be safe and still be wrong because it is "coercive, debasing, harmful, or cruel to another."[27] Just as the fact that sex is monogamous does not necessarily make it right, so the fact that it is safe does not necessarily make it right.

Moreover, while the safety of one's *partner* should certainly be a concern for anyone practicing Christian sexual morality, self-sacrificial love is a human possibility. Safety of *oneself* has always been understood in Christian tradition as less than the fullness of love.[28]

Safe sex, then, is not necessarily moral sex. This is partly because safe sex is linked to fear and self-protectiveness. Fear is non-Christian, even anti-Christian. To reestablish a sexual ethic based on fear is to permit Christian values to be submerged into cultural values that are at root antithetical to the Christian message.

What Do We Teach?

Two elements are needed for a valid Christian sexual ethic in the face of the AIDS epidemic. One is an adequate understanding of the virus that transmits susceptability to AIDS and of the com-

---

[25] "John," quoted by Shelp et al., *AIDS: Personal Stories*, p. 94.

[26] After noting that 100 gay men gather in safe sex clubs to "jerk off" together, Armistead Maupin declares that their behavior is "perfectly safe and perfectly moral." It may be perfectly safe; but is it perfectly moral?

[27] The United Church of Christ, *Human Sexuality: A Preliminary Study* (N.Y.: United Church Press, 1977), p. 104.

[28] Some gay men wittingly risk their own health by making love to their infected partners, choosing to affirm love over death.

munities at risk for AIDS. As with the transmission of any virus, AIDS raises public health issues and a concern for safety.

The more central element necessary for a Christian sexual ethic in the face of the AIDS epidemic is an appropriation of Christian values. A Christian ethic does not — indeed, cannot — consist in a list of "do's" and "don't's" intended to protect ourselves and make sex safe. Concern for the practice of safe sex is legitimate and has its place in a Christian ethic. But an exclusive focus on safe sex is not an adequate Christian sexual ethic. The concern for safety brings fear. Fear is easily turned into blame and scapegoating.

Fear and scapegoating are not Christian approaches to our neighbor. It is, therefore, fundamentally a theological issue, argues Nelson, when those seeking after security do so through the "false" mechanism of rejecting all who appear to embody their insecurities. He proposes a response "from the heart of the Christian gospel." "To those whose insecurity is so painful that they must find scapegoats on whom to lay blame for all anxieties and evil," suggests Nelson, "there is that One who demonstrates the triumph of grace announcing that all are free to live as those who are accepted."[29]

Love and acceptance are fundamental to the Christian gospel. In our desire for "safe sex," we must be sure that we have not lost the heart of the gospel, which is love.

Dr. Lebacqz is professor of Christian ethics at Pacific School of Religion.
Ms. Blake is a doctoral candidate in moral theology at the Graduate Theological Union in Berkeley, California.

---

[29] Nelson, *Between Two Gardens*, p. 152.

LEARNING FIDELITY: THE PEDAGOGY OF WATCHFUL CARE

Kenneth Vaux

University of Illinois
Chicago, Illinois

I

> "Behold I will send you Elijah the prophet before the coming of the great and dreadful day of the Lord; And he shall turn the heart of the fathers to the children, and the heart of the children to their fathers, lest I come and smite the earth with a curse" (Malachi 4: 5-6).

"Smite the earth with a curse!" "How ridiculous!" Nature doesn't bestow reward or bring revenge like that, or does it? We all know that what we call nature — the physical universe — is orderly, predictable, and absolutely indiscriminate. Surely it follows Newton's serene laws. Judgment — the commendation of good and condemnation of evil — is not a natural process. Atoms and molecules, microbes and animals, these follow their built-in ordained and random processes. "Mother nature" is as ridiculous a notion as "wrathful God" — or is it?

The disease AIDS has entered the human world through a rupture in the ecology membrane. Whatever its origins (perhaps the African green monkey is the culprit vector), like syphilis in the sixteenth century a new plague has entered the Western world, and again it is out of Africa and Haiti. "The AIDS pandemic" writes Stephen Jay Gould, the Harvard biologist, "an issue that may rank with nuclear weaponry as the greatest danger of our era, provides a more striking proof that mind and technology are not omnipotent and that we have not cancelled our bond to nature."[1]

---

[1] Stephen Jay Gould, "The Terrifying Normalcy of AIDS," *The New York Times Magazine*, April 19, 1987, p. 33.

Surely there is an insensibility to nature's warning in our procrastination and failure to get serious about AIDS. We did not heed the alarm that sounded from Africa more than a decade ago. The point of "innoculation" was scarcely noted on the global health surveillance screens. Even today our state of concern is far less than it should be, because it is appearing first among the poor, blacks, Haitians, gays, drug abusers, prostitutes, and the other despised and forgotten persons in our world. It's out there, beyond the pale, outside the camp. We can wait it out, and indeed we may. Although blacks are only 12 percent of the U.S. population, they represent 25 percent of all adult cases, 50 percent of the cases in women, and 53 percent of the child cases.[2] The rupture of AIDS into our apathetic world has come at the thin point of membrane breakage down in the pockets of acute pain where dereliction is their cry back to our "I don't give a damn about you" kind of world. The AIDS crisis is a cry for reeducation of the human heart.

A poignant illustration of how AIDS has torn the delicate fabric of our social existence recently came to light in Chicago. The victim, twin brother of a straight, conservative, homophobic young man and son of a mother with similar intense emotional and political feelings, had to confront both of them with the fact that he was gay, had AIDS, and was dying. The awful, soul-shaking upheaval of beliefs, values, and loyalties faced in the microcosm of this family is now faced in the drama of fidelity confronting our society. The focal point of this soul-searching, involving value and belief clarification, as well as understandings and commitments, will occur within the structures of moral education: the school, church, and family. The crisis of AIDS compels us to a new pedagogy about fidelity, lest we lapse into a response of condemnation and forgetfulness and, in that withdrawal, lose our own soul.

Today the magnitude of the AIDS problem is at long last coming into focus. Most of the countries of the world, including the thought-to-be impervious China and Russia, now have cases reported. As of mid-year 1987, there are 50,000 reported cases worldwide. With the poor reporting mechanisms of African states, we may assume that there are twice that many. Dr. Jonathan Mann of the World Health Organization projects that be-

---

[2] George E. Curry, "More AIDS Help Urged for Blacks," *Chicago Tribune*, Wed., July 23, 1987, sec. 1, p. 5.

tween 500,000 and three million people will develop AIDS by 1992. In the United States, Dr. James Curran of the Communicable Disease Centers, reports that 36,000 people have had AIDS and over 21,000 have already died from it. He estimates that between 1 and 1.5 million are now infected with the virus, a great portion of whom will die. In New York City, already the major cause of death in young women (20-40 years) is AIDS. Some estimates hold that one man out of every 30 in this age range is infected.[3] But should alarm be translated into moral indignation or smug satisfaction? Gould goes on to caution us when we moralize about plagues:

> We must also grasp the perspective of ecology and evolutionary biology and recognize, once we reinsert ourselves properly into nature, that AIDS represents the ordinary workings of biology, not an irrational or diabolical plague with moral meaning . . . AIDS is a natural phenomenon, one of a recurring class of pandemic diseases. Yes, AIDS may run through the entire population, and may carry off a quarter or more of us. Yet, it may make no *biological* difference to Homo Sapiens in the long run: There will still be plenty of us left and we can start again. Evolution cares as little for its agents — organisms struggling for reproductive success — as physics cares for individual atoms of hydrogen in the sun. But *we* care. These atoms are our neighbors, our lovers, our children, and ourselves. AIDS is a natural phenomenon and, potentially, the greatest natural tragedy in human history.[4]

It is indeed in the realm of relationships, not in sheer nature itself, that the moral dimension begins to arise. Nature itself is not a placid reality, it agonizes, as we have argued, and evokes moral sympathies. But, as Gould might agree, it is in the connectedness and reciprocity in nature's web, in the delight of coherence and purpose and in the pains of disjunction and damage that nature becomes a part of the human moral world.

It is at this point that we can call the coming into our life of pathologic AIDS as a disease, a moral crisis. AIDS represents a breach in the customary non-virulence of the microbial world. We have come to expect that the micro-organisms of the lifeworld will occupy their own niche, exert their specific generational vitality and their natural populational dynamics and not reach out destructively into the rest of nature. AIDS indeed may be an unnatural intrusion into the stratum of human life, perhaps

---

[3] "AIDS: Statistics but Few Answers," *Science*, vol., 236, no. 4807, 12 June 1987, p. 1423-1425.

[4] Gould, *OP. CIT*, p. 30.

overwhelming the compromised host organism in the same way that natural, benign flora in the body become destructive to persons whose resistance is defective or compromised. Patients with Severe Combined Immunological Deficiency (SCID), cancer, and those who have undergone transplants and whose bone marrow has been irradiated are examples of such host compromise.

The fact that AIDS has exerted its virulence at the point where humans are behaving in morally questionable ways — homosexuality, especially compulsive and promiscuous homosexuality; contaminated needle drug abuse; prostitution and other aberrant human encounters where "bodily fluids" are exchanged in uncommon ways — gives rise to moral opprobrium. That innocent children (hemophiliacs of which 90 percent are now infected with AIDS), the unborn and newborn offspring of infected mothers, and innocent spouses are infected confounds this moral backlash and creates a different moral appraisal. In this case, the assumption of innocence yields a more concerted effort to be of help. At this point we see the need for revival of the old moral pedagogy, that which predated the libertarian educational ethos that Alan Bloom describes in *The Closing of the American Mind*. This new world of toleration and open-mindedness, where no one believes anything and one value or lifestyle is thought to be as good as another, is at the root of our crisis. The old pedagogy commends fidelity like the father of the prodigal son, even when the son has gone astray. The grace of hating the sin but loving the sinner is possible only in the forgiven and redeemed conscience. Today we have witnessed the breakdown of what our deepest religious traditions have found to be "the good life" or "the way of life" (chaste, faithful, monogamous, and heterosexual). This breakdown has flourished from the 1960s forward in America. The new pattern of sexual behavior has unleashed the plagues that we gather under the rubric STDs (sexually transmitted diseases), which include syphyilis, gonorrhea, PID (Pelvic Inflamatory Disease), chlamydia, and now AIDS.

The release of the licentious "do your own thing" ethic was preceded by a loss of vitality in the traditional biblical sex ethic as it degenerated into a pathological puritanism.

The story and film, *Dr. Strangelove or How I Learned to Love the Bomb*, parodied, in the figure of USA Air Force Commander Jack D. Ripper, the paranoid fear that communist forces, floridation, ar.d all new that scares us were out to deplete and contaminate our "vital bodily fluids." Such films and books, indeed all the reactions and counter-reactions of the "free love" movement of the 1960s and 1970s, betrayed our concern that human sexual activity be viewed in moral terms but that we not return to Victorian prudery.

If we are to relearn the grace of watchful care or fidelity in a world that is rapidly polarizing into the camps of retributive moralizing and indulgent hedonizing, we will need to become prudent but not prudish. We must again be taught faith attitudes, that is, postures of waiting, watching, being there, and remaining. Dr. Rieux, in Camus' *The Plague*, and Father Damien among the Lepers of Molokai are living figures who "stand out" in this posture. They abide amid threat. They stand up to the common person's prejudice and hatred. The quality they embody is a subtle but powerful willingness to take a risk, to participate in trial, and to bear pain and suffering with another. In the Christian story, Peter the Apostle comes close. While the other disciples fall asleep and slide away on that fateful evening, he at least lingers on, hovers in the shadows, even though he finally himself turns the whole thing off and flees.

The posture contrary to watchful care, the negentropic as opposed to the tropic ethic, is revulsion, disregard, and withdrawal. The police, ambulance driver, and even the mortician in *The Normal Heart*, a great drama on AIDS, refuse to come near, to touch, or to identify with the victim. This should not surprise us because it is the natural response to the "awful." Rudolf Otto, in *The Idea of the Holy*, showed how an awesome experience, the primal perception of mystery, evokes both attraction and repulsion, both endearment and dread. We need to be trained in the pedagogy of the soul toward identification, involvement, and amelioration. We need to be led away from the propensity to deny, repress, and flee, unless shunning is the only response that can heal and restore.

The AIDS crisis is provoking this kind of disruption and call in our moral souls today. The call for help is the call to alleviate, if possible; but if not, to abide in the presence of suffering. This means, in the first place, doing everything we can to prevent the occurrence of AIDS. This means the nurturing of wholesome lifestyles, ways of life in accord with the prophylactic ethics of our tradition. It means fostering vigorous educational programs and emergency prophylaxis in a world that we know has gone astray. It means drawing near in support when the disease strikes. This last measure of sharing suffering entails funding research, supporting nondiscrimination, non-retaliative policy in the work place, at school, and in public services. It means finding ways to provide AZT and other costly medication, making available excellent clinical care, and finally insuring dignified terminal and hospice care.

II

Three moral characteristics of a fidelity-tempered ethic and pedagogy that will serve us throughout the coming decades of the AIDS crisis will be (1) thoughtful patience at the inception of this dread pandemic; (2) grave seriousness about the potency of sex in this world that has made it so casual; and (3) the careful yet serene preparation for the Armageddon-like struggle that faces us.

1. Often an apocalypse can be averted or blunted in its force. The AIDS epidemic may be demolished in its tracks by a powerful prophylactic vaccination or a sophisticated therapy. Research breakthroughs in the coming years may make this possible. This dramatic rescue, however, is unlikely. We will probably need the waiting of thoughtful, abiding patience at the outset of this pandemic to diminish its devastation as much as possible.

In an important article exploring the modifications to behavior among the heterosexual community in response to the AIDS alarm, Peter Davis writes

> Since it is primarily contracted through sex and the use of drugs, two activities associated both with desire and free will, AIDS tests us as no disease ever has. It is the first plague in the history of mankind whose regulation is entirely dependent upon our knowing behavior.[5]

Three relatively untested powers of the moral psyche are now being challenged by the AIDS crisis. Some people know they do not have the disease. They may feel smug, even gleeful, at the misfortune of others or, at best, cautious about themselves, their relationship with others, and the provision of a safer society for their fellows. These people need to translate their gratitude, "there but for the grace of God go I," into sacrificial care for those who are afflicted. Second, there are many, perhaps millions, of people who do not know whether or not they have been infected or whether they will succumb to the disease. This unusual state of apprehension — not knowing for sure if one has been exposed but

---

[5] Peter Davis, "Exploring the Kingdom of AIDS," *The New York Times Magazine*, May 31, 1987, p. 32.

has not yet developed antibody titers — this veiled ignorance calls for a special kind of patience, trust, and faithfulness. A third group knows that though death may be delayed, it is inevitable. Such persons need to know of society's acceptance and care so they can be relieved of fear, even vengeful anger, tempting them to infect others as they die. Forgiveness one to the other is the absolute imperative during this death watch. The dying have always been our best teachers about the meaning of life. Our fidelity can restore their fidelity in the covenant of reciprocal wisdom. This is the essence of pedagogy.

2. The AIDS crisis is causing us to become acutely aware, as were our primitive forebears, of the awesome potency of sexual power. Davis continues:

> In the kingdom of AIDS a penis itself, often linked to a sword in folktales (a smoking gun in current political parlance), again becomes a deadly weapon . . . Since our perception of threat presumably determines our behavior, perhaps only an exaggerated depiction of the danger AIDS now poses for heterosexuals will prevent that worse-case scenario from ultimately becoming the reality. It seems paradoxical; but the result is we are being warned that we are all bombs and some of our fuses have been lighted.[6]

In a world where images of potency have been emasculated and displaced by casual and technical images, this perception comes as a shock.

In the primitive and ancient world, the awesome potency of sexual power became the basis for comparing one's potency and fertility with the very creative power of the gods. The moral significance was that we then exerted this power with awesome respect. The strictures against misguided sex and against perverted sex (turned away from proper goals) emerged from this sublime sense that human recreation and procreation were in some sense identified with the divine potency. The fact that we now know both the deleterious microbes that voyage along the conjugal channels (AIDS) and the "good viruses" that may indeed safeguard against disease has further enhanced this reawakened moral sense that sex is important and not trivial. The biblical tradition of sexual ethics contends that the *Imago Dei*, the most central spiritual and moral capacity of the soul, is found in male and female being together.

---

[6] Ibid., p. 34.

In the image of God he created them male and female he created them.

Genesis I

3. Finally, a pedagogy of fidelity fosters a readiness to endure a long struggle of good and evil, hope and disappointment. The symbols of an agonizing, intractable conflict in which a people are sustained in comfort by an expectation of deliverance, all the while bolstered by the staying power of service, are the moral symbols of our moral heritage and relevant to the AIDS ordeal (see Isaiah: 40). Davis concludes

> In this respect, the threat of AIDS is not unlike that of nuclear annihilation. In both cases, the will to act, either personally or collectively, must be preceded by a perceived and immediate danger. With AIDS, that perception is rising among us. A generation ago a president, speaking of the cold war, warned Americans they were in for a long twilight struggle. He might as well have been predicting AIDS.[7]

The immediate moral quandaries about AIDS — Shall testing be required or only offered? Shall records be kept confidential? Shall public interests override personal liberties? Shall doctors and nurses be required to offer care? Shall infected or diseased persons lose their rights to certain protection? Shall infected children be admitted to school? Shall volatile drugs be made available faster by circumventing research regulations? Shall recuscitation be offered or withheld from AIDS patients who arrest? — all these and myriad other present and future ethical questions are subsumed and directed by the more basic issues of a society's fundamental commitments. The main ethical issue at stake in the AIDS crisis is our faithfulness. The true test will come in our fiduciary covenants of life with life and our ability to teach these commandments to our children.

III

The medical profession in its internal ethics has struggled with the pedagogy of sustaining care in the face of danger. In 1847, when the first AMA code was published, a small companion booklet held that during epidemics

> . . . and when pestilence prevails, it is their (physicians') duty to face the danger, and to continue their labors for the alleviation of the suffering, even at the jeopardy of their own lives.[8]

---

[7] Ibid., p. 40.

[8] The American Medical Association, *Code of Ethics of the American Medical Association.* (Philadelphia: Turner Hamilton, 1981), p. 32.

This document, growing out of the pious and pastoral commitments of medicine in the early nineteenth century (e.g., see Percival's Code) was clinically naive in knowledge about antisepsis and asepsis but compassionate to the sick as expressed in the willingness to suffer and die for another, even holding near someone who was contaminated. Today, again, we need Mother Theresas. When we witness Catholic sisters caring for the sick with complete disregard for their own protection or see Father Damien working faithfully among those whom he could finally call "my fellow lepers," we are reminded of an ethic of love long lost to our pragmatic world but the only ethic that can save and heal.

Today the AMA code is silent on the ethics of exposure and risk. At the end of 1986, the AMA issued a statement on physicians' responsibilities toward patients with AIDS, which reflects the more libertarian, noncommunal ethos of our time. Although the document acknowledged the long history of self-sacrifice in the presence of suffering and the historic commitment to be with contagious patients, it counseled: "A physician shall, in the provision of appropriate patient care, except in emergencies, be free to choose whom to serve."[9] This swing of position reflects a basic change in the moral mandate of medicine, now much more a technical occupation and entrepeneurial opportunity than a pastoral obligation. Today, medicine, the ministry, indeed all the professions of help and care are challenged along with the entire human community to reclaim fidelity or further descend into the hell of forgetfulness.

We have summarily reviewed the moral nature of the AIDS crisis and found the essence of the crisis to be an occasion for moral responsibility. We have shown that fidelity, perhaps even more than beneficence or justice, is the cardinal virtue called into question. We have shown that restoration of faithfulness is the best hope for enduring and overcoming this crisis with grace and civility. AIDS has opened up this chasm, this crisis, this occasion for renewal or damnation.

Dr. Vaux is professor of ethics in medicine, University of Illinois at Chicago.

---

[9] Report of the Council on Ethical and Judical Affairs Statement on AIDS. *American Medical Association*, Dec. 1, 1986.

THE PERSPECTIVE OF JEWISH TEACHING

Ronald M. Green

Dartmouth College
Hanover, N.H. 03755

The Jewish tradition contains a complex body of teaching, stretching back for almost three millennia, on matters of medicine and medical ethics. As we might expect, much of this teaching deals with the problem of epidemic infectious diseases, since these have always been among the most serious threats to health. In the face of the AIDS epidemic, it is interesting and useful to review this body of Jewish teaching. While some aspects of traditional teaching may have been rendered irrelevant by modern medical knowledge or by changing ethical values, others can help shed light on some of the perplexing moral and religious problems posed by AIDS.

Traditional Jewish attitudes to the threat of infectious diseases and epidemics may be grouped around two distinct and seemingly opposing poles. At one extreme, we find the position that places a premium on self-protection, avoidance, and even flight in response to the risk of infection. At the other extreme, we find themes of compassion, of reaching out, and of dedicated service to those who fall victim to contagious disease. Although these responses are potentially in deep conflict, we will see that they have frequently been harmonized in Jewish life and teaching. In addition, the special qualities of the AIDS epidemic seem to yield a fairly uniform Jewish response to the ethical challenges posed by AIDS. As I develop each of these broad categories of response, I will relate them to the AIDS issue by extrapolating from the traditional teaching and by indicating positions taken by contemporary Jewish thinkers.

Themes of Self-Protection, Avoidance, and Flight

Among the contagious diseases discussed in traditional Jewish sources, leprosy perhaps furnished the closest parallel to AIDS. Because of its irregular pattern of infection, delayed onset, and inevitably gruesome progression, leprosy was greatly feared, and lepers were normally subject to isolation or avoidance.[1] In the Jewish sources, this response finds its most graphic expression in a passage in the Bible commentaries (Midrash Rabbah) that records the attitudes of several venerated sages to this disease and its victims:

> R. Johanan and Resh Lakish stated that it is forbidden to walk four cubits, or 100 cubits (dependent upon whether there was a wind blowing at the time) to the east of a leper; R. Meir refrained from eating eggs which came from a district where lepers lived; R. Ammi and R. Assi never entered such a district; when Resh Lakish saw one he would cast stones at them, exclaiming, "get back to your location and do not contaminate other people"; and R. Eleazer b. Simeon would hide from them.[2]

Because of its apparently uncharitable spirit, this kind of teaching has proven embarrassing to some modern Jewish commentators.[3] To some extent, this embarrassment is well founded, since rabbinic attitudes toward contagious diseases in general, and to leprosy in particular, sometimes display an irrational and punitive quality. In much Jewish (and biblical) teaching, for example, there is a tendency to regard disease and epidemics as divine retribution for individuals' or communities' sins; and leprosy itself, through a series of fanciful etymologies and biblical references, was sometimes viewed by the rabbis as punishment for the sins of slander or libel.[4] Applied to the AIDS epidemic, this mentality, combined with the many biblical and rabbinic condemnations of homosexual conduct,[5] might easily lead to a posi-

---

[1] For a review of Jewish teaching on this matter, see the entry on "Leprosy" in the *Encyclopedia Judaica*, vol. 11, cols. 33-39.

[2] Leviticus Rabbah. 16:3. Quoted in Ibid., col. 38.

[3] See, for example, the Kol Nidre sermon delivered by Rabbi Robert Kirschner at Temple Emmanuel in San Francisco and distributed by the Union of American Hebrew Congregations, as part of its packet, "Confronting the AIDS Crisis" (UAHC Committee on AIDS, 838 Fifth Avenue, New York, N.Y. 10021. New York).

[4] *Encyclopedia Judaica*, "Leprosy," col. 38.

[5] Traditional Jewish teaching, drawing on the prohibitions and punishments in Leviticus 18:22 and 20:13, regards homosexual conduct between males as an "abomination" (*to-evah*) and prescribes the penalty of death. This prohibition and punishment are reaffirmed in the Talmud (Mishnah Sanhedrin 7:4). Discussions of traditional teaching in this area

tion adopted by some conservative Christian spokespeople who regard AIDS as a divine punishment, view AIDS sufferers as deserved victims of their own sins, and advocate a return to traditional sexual and moral values as the most important response to the crisis.

Nevertheless, this kind of punitive attitude has not been pronounced in recent Jewish responses to the AIDS epidemic. As we will see, Jewish spokespeople, whether they belong to the Orthodox, Conservative, or Reform branches of the tradition, have tended to mute these themes of retribution and have generally refused to use this crisis as an opportunity to reiterate traditional teachings on homosexuality. Part of the reason is the presence of the themes of compassion, which we will soon explore. But part also is the fact that even the less charitable attitudes of avoidance and isolation evidenced in the traditional literature have their roots, not just in punitive ideas, but also in the very strong emphasis in traditional teaching on the duty of self-preservation and the maintenance of one's health. Although this emphasis did lead to admonitions to self-protection in circumstances of epidemics or plague, it did not necessarily imply hostility or punishment for those neighbors unfortunate enough to fall victim to disease.

The emphasis on self-protection grows out of the extremely heavy emphasis traditional Jewish teaching places on the value of human life. The Jewish attitude is eloquently summed up in a talmudic passage regarding the creation of Adam:

> Therefore only a single human being was created in the world, to teach that if any person has caused a single soul of Israel to perish, Scripture regards him as if he had caused an entire world to perish; and if any human being saves a single soul of Israel, scripture regards him as if he had saved an entire world.[6]

In Jewish teaching on medical care, this same attitude was applied to each individual's responsbility for his or her own physical well-being. Commenting on the biblical passages *take heed to thyself, and take care to thy life* (Deut. 4:9) and *take good care of*

---

include Norman Lamm, "Judaism and the Modern Attitude to Homosexuality," in Fred Rosner and J. David Bleich, eds., *Jewish Bioethics* (New York: Sanhedrin Press, 1979), pp. 197-218 and the symposium "Homosexuals and Homosexuality: Psychiatrists, Religious Leaders and Laymen Compare Notes," *Judaism* 32:4 (Fall 1983), pp. 390-443. Alone among the branches of Judaism, the Reform movement has moved to an acceptance of homosexuality. Its synagogue organization, the Union of American Hebrew Congregations, numbers four gay congregations in its membership.

   [6] Babylonian Talmud, Sanhedrin, 37a.

your lives (Deut. 4:15), rabbinic commentators concluded that each person has a positive duty to protect himself or herself from harm or disease. It is this series of teachings, not merely irrational condemnation or fear, that inspired the repeated rabbinic admonitions to flee from plague environments or to be wary of possible sources of contagion.[7]

This same valuation of human life and sense of moral obligation to self-care also underlay the early Jewish permission for medical therapies. As many commentators have noted, religious traditions, which rely on God's providential governance of life as do Judaism and its daughter traditions, have a tendency to regard sickness as a divinely willed condition and have a corresponding tendency to resist medical interventions. This impulse has shown itself more than once in Christianity and also made an appearance in Jewish sectarian movements.[8] Nevertheless, from the earliest date, the normative Jewish tradition decisively rejected this response. Although God was viewed as the ultimate source of healing, medical efforts in general and efforts of the physician in particular were viewed as valid forms of human assistance in the healing process.[9] The firm rabbinic teaching over the centuries was that, although in biblical times God may have directly caused and removed disease, "nowadays one must not rely on miracles."[10] Applied to the AIDS epidemic, this attitude and teaching militates against retreat to religious homilies or diatribes in response to a major health threat. Judaism's longstanding tradition of "medical rationalism," a tradition that from the earliest date permitted violation of the Sabbath whenever needed to save or protect a human life, seems to have little room for castigating the victims or potential victims of a lethal malady.

Jewish insistence on the protection and preservation of human life (the duty of *pikku'ah nefesh*) also has implications for the conduct and obligations of medical practitioners during times of medical emergency, and some of these may have relevance to the AIDS epidemic. Just as it greatly valued the services of physicians

---

[7] Hence the teaching in the Babylonian Talmud (Baba Kamma, 60b): "When the plague is in town, gather your legs."

[8] For a discussion of these matters see Immanuel Jakobovits, *Jewish Medical Ethics* (New York: Bloch Publishing Company, 1959), ch. 1.

[9] Babylonian Talmud, Baba Kamma, 85a.

[10] The eighteenth-century rabbi Chayim Azulai, quoted in Fred Rosner, *Modern Medicine and Jewish Law* (New York: Bloch Publishing Company, 1972), p 24.

— many of the more famous rabbis, like Maimonides, were physicians themselves — Judaism also imposed obligations on the doctor and other health workers when they were in a special position to save life. Thus, in contrast to ordinary citizens — who, in keeping with the duty of self-preservation, were encouraged to flee epidemics and plagues — physicians had a special duty to care for their patients, even at some measure of personal risk to themselves. In Joseph Karo's important eighteenth-century code of Jewish law, we read the following: "The Torah gave permission to the physician to heal; moreover, this is a religious precept and is included in the category of saving life; and if the physician withholds his services it is considered as shedding blood."[11] In an adjacent passage of this code, Karo also condemned a physician's withdrawal from medical practice, even if other physicians are available, "since a man is not [always] destined to be healed by any [random] person."[12]

Interestingly, the physician's responsibility in this area was not regarded in Jewish law (*Halakhah*) as deriving from any special professional duties of the physician. On the basis of the biblical text, "Nor shall you stand idly by the blood of your fellow" (Leviticus 19:16), the Talmud taught that any human being was morally obligated to come to the aid of a neighbor in peril.[13] At the same time, the duty of self-protection was taken so seriously in Judaism that there was always a great hesitancy to permit or allow acts of assistance to others that placed one's own life in jeopardy.[14] If physicians and related health care workers were required to serve during times of plague, therefore, this was not because they had special professional obligations that exempted them from the duty of self-regard. Rather, it was because of the view that such individuals were able to protect themselves sufficiently from infection so that the danger to themselves was reduced to a level where the duty of assistance would override the duty of self-protection.

The question of whether physicians are obligated to treat

---

[11] Yoreh De'ah 336:1. Quoted in J. David Bleich, *Judaism and Healing* (New York: Ktav, 1981), p. 4.

[12] Quoted in Jakobovits, *Jewish Medical Ethics*, p. 211.

[13] Babylonian Talmud, Sanhedrin, 73a.

[14] For a review of Jewish teaching on the duty of beneficence and its differences, especially in the area of medical ethics, from Christian teaching, see my "Jewish Ethics and Beneficence," in Earl Shelp, ed., *Beneficence and Health Care* (Dordrecht: D. Reidel, 1982), pp. 109-125.

AIDS patients (or those who are seropositive for HIV) has generated one of the most heated controversies in the AIDS epidemic. Although the details of a technical rabbinic ruling in this area might well change as our medical knowledge evolves, so long as it is possible for health care workers to provide a substantial measure of protection for themselves against the risk of infection, we can say that the traditional Jewish encouragement to flight from epidemics would appear not to pertain to physicians, who would be required under traditional law to continue to render their services to patients in need.[15]

The Jewish understanding of the duty to protect life might also have bearing on the complex issue of AIDS reporting. As Rabbi Immanuel Jakobovits observes in his authoritative study of Jewish medical ethics, "the only clause in the Hippocratic Oath altogether ignored in Jewish law concerns the undertaking to guard professional secrets."[16] Although this peculiarity of Jewish teaching has several bases (including the belief that the physician's duty of confidentiality was adequately comprised under the prohibitions against slander or gossip), it also derives from the Jewish position that where risk to human life is involved, the protection of privacy must take a subordinate place in our concern. Hence, in Jewish teaching it was held to be a physician's duty to report a patient's physical and even emotional problems to a prospective mate if these problems might jeopardize the future partner's life or health.[17]

As Rabbi J. David Bleich observes, Jewish law also provides that a rabbinic court or *Bet Din* "may compel testimony which entails revelation of a personal or professional confidence. The obligation born of the commandment '. . . he who is a witness . . . if he does not inform, he shall bear his iniquity' (Leviticus 5:1) supersedes the obligation to respect the privacy of others." Bleich adds that "in such instances Jewish law would require that testimony of this nature be heard *in camera* in order that matters of a personal nature not be overheard by persons who have no 'need to know.' "[18]

---

[15] I am indebted on this matter to insight provided me by Rabbi Moses Tendler, University Professor of Medical Ethics at Yeshiva University in New York.

[16] *Jewish Medical Ethics*, p. 210.

[17] The issue of disclosure of medical information is discussed in detail in the *Chafetz Chaim*, a classic work dealing with Jewish law as applied to slander, defamation of character, and gossip. For a discussion of this text and the issues it raises, see Bleich, *Judaism and Healing*, pp. 34-36.

[18] Ibid., p. 36.

The issue of AIDS testing and the related matter of disclosure of information gathered through testing or medical treatment are enormously complex. Policy analysis in this area must pit the immediate benefit accrued to the public through this information (especially where the protection of possible sexual partners is concerned) against the invasions of privacy and the very serious "chilling effect" any program of required testing and disclosure would have on the willingness of possible HIV carriers to report for testing or treatment.[19] Without even trying to settle this issue here, I can suggest that traditional Jewish teaching seems to favor the disclosure of confidential medical information, even at some loss to privacy, where this might clearly minimize the risk to human life. Jewish teaching would also favor the control of such disclosure and the limitation of confidential information to those clearly having a "need to know." I might add that this approach appears to inform the stances of some Reform synagogue organizations on the matter of how religious schools should handle HIV-infected students. A recent policy statement on this issue by the (Reform) Union of American Hebrew Congregations, for example, rules out the mass testing of children or employees in synagogue schools but, where a child has knowingly been infected with the virus, permits the sharing of this information with administrators or teachers on a "need to know" basis.[20]

The Jewish insistence on the duties of saving life (*pikku'ah nefesh*) and self-protection have several further implications for the AIDS epidemic. The importance of the first of these duties, for example, would appear to leave no doubt that individuals infected with the HIV virus who knowingly risk other persons by unsafe sexual or drug practices are not only in violation of stern ethical requirements but also may be subject to legal control and restraint. The second duty would place a corresponding obligation on individuals to protect themselves from the risk of infection. Although traditional Judaism prohibits homosexual behavior and even heterosexual sex outside a marital context, and

---

[19] A balanced position on these issues has been taken by the joint Health and Public Policy Committee of the American College of Physicians and Infectious Diseases Society of America (1986). For a discussion of this, see Lewis H. Kuller and Lawrence A. Kingsley, "The Epidemic of AIDS: A Failure of Public Health Policy," *Milbank Quarterly*, Vol. 64, Suppl. 1, 1986, 73.

[20] Union of American Hebrew Congregations, "Recommendations for Children and Employees with Acquired Immune Deficiency Syndrome/HIV Infection in the Synagogue Setting," published in the packet of information "Confronting the AIDS Crisis."

although some orthodox commentators would certainly disagree with me, I believe it is a legitimate extension of traditional Jewish teaching to hold that, in the circumstances of the present medical crisis, the encouragement to "safe sex" in educational approaches to the AIDS epidemic takes precedence over moralistic encouragements to abstinence. I am not just saying that this balancing of priorities makes sense given modern attitudes and values. It seems to me a valid extrapolation from Judaism's own long tradition of medical rationalism and concern for life and health.

Themes of Compassion

If cautious self-protection constitutes one pole of Jewish teaching about infectious disease, themes of fellow-feeling and encouragements to generous support and assistance to those who suffer constitute the other. Furthermore, just as talmudic passages, like the one dealing with the rabbis' fearful response to leprosy, can be quoted to illustrate one pole of this teaching, so can passages be quoted that evidence these themes of compassion. Two passages in particular come to mind. One recounts a fuller range of the sages' response to the leper's plight:

> R. Zera never sat with such a sufferer in the same draught. R. Eleazar never entered his tent. R. Ammi and R. Assi never ate any of the eggs coming from the alley in which he lived. R. Joshua b. Levi, however, attached himself to these sufferers and studied the Torah, for he said, [the Torah is] *A lovely hind and a graceful doe* (Prov. 5: 19). If the Torah bestows grace upon those who study it, would it not also protect them?[21]

Although Rabbi Joshua b. Levi might have been motivated as much by his confidence in the quasi-magical protection afforded by the study of Torah as he was by sympathy with lepers, there can be no doubt that his compassion was also valued for itself. A second talmudic passage also involves this saintly rabbi, and, fancifully, it presents him interrogating no less an authority than the prophet Elijah about how we shall locate the messiah when he arrives:

> "Where," R. Joshua asked, "shall I find the Messiah?"
> "At the gate of the city," Elijah replied.
> "How shall I recognize him?"
> "He sits among the lepers."

---

[21] Babylonian Talmud, Kethuboth, 77b.

"Among the lepers!" cried R. Joshua: "What is he doing there?"
"He changes their bandages," Elijah answered, "He changes them one
by one."[22]

In traditional Jewish teaching and culture, this sentiment did
not remain merely at the level of homily. The obligation to visit
the sick (the duty of *bikkur holim*) was one of the most strenu-
ously enjoined and observed. God himself was said to have observed this *mitzvah* when he visited Abraham who was recover-
ing from his circumcision (Gen. 18:1), and the divine presence
was said to hover above the invalid's bed.[23] Because of God's special solicitousness for the infirm, the precept of *bikkur holim* was
regarded as one of the commandments for which "a man enjoys
the fruits in this world while the principal remains for him in the
world to come."[24]

In rabbinic teaching, merely visiting the sick was not regarded
as the true fulfillment of this *mitzvah*. The sick person had also to
be aided and his or her material needs satisfied. For this reason,
traditional Jewish communities established various associations
(societies for *bikkur holim* and burial organizations, *hevra kaddi-
sha*) whose task it was to visit the sick, attend to the needs of dying
patients, and prepare the body of the deceased for burial. These
organizations not only provided these services, they also furnished material support and saw that medical services were available to those without means. In both personal and practical ways,
therefore, Jews were enjoined to let the sick person know that he
or she was not left alone in this moment of pain and suffering.[25]

The application of this deep tradition of teaching and communal service to the context of AIDS is obvious. If we keep in mind
the fact that AIDS is not a disease communicable by casual contact and, therefore, one to which the duty of flight for self-
protection is not relevant, traditional Jewish teaching points to a
positive obligation of social and communal care for AIDS victims.
The recent appeals by some Reform Jewish organizations for
"warm support and sympathy" for AIDS victims and their families and their advocacy of synagogue-based "buddy systems" to

---

[22] Babylonian Talmud, Sanhedrin, 98a. My attention was drawn to this passage by
Rabbi Kirschner's Kol Nidre sermon. See above, n. 3.

[23] Babylonian Talmud, Nedarim, 40a.

[24] For a discussion of these teachings see the entry "Sick, Visiting the," *Encyclopedia
Judaica*, vol. 14, cols. 1496-8.

[25] Ibid., col. 1497.

comfort and sustain AIDS patients strike me as exemplary modern expressions of these ancient Jewish teachings.[26] Equally relevant in the context of our complex modern society are political efforts aimed at insuring the societal provision of medical coverage for AIDS sufferers, practices of nondiscrimination in employment and housing, and unstinting commitment to research into the causes and cures of this malady. Despite the amenities of modern life, it is no less easy than it has ever been to be left "alone" in the hour of sickness and death. The spirit of the ancient precept of *bikkur holim*, in both its personal and practical dimensions, seems to me one of Judaism's most important contributions to our response to AIDS.

Concluding Remarks

Traditional Jewish teaching about infectious disease was formed in a context very different from our own. It would be inappropriate to take any one aspect of this tradition and apply it, without deliberation, to a malady as complex as AIDS. Nevertheless, I have suggested that some of the deepest motifs of this tradition, motifs that transcend specific diseases like leprosy or specific sexual-moral teachings, can help guide our thinking in these new circumstances. These motifs include the tradition's extreme solicitousness to human life and health, its overwhelmingly rational and realistic response to medical emergencies, and its compassion, consistent with the urgent needs of communal self-protection, to those who suffer disease.

I want to close, however, with one additional reflection. Among other things, for the time being, the AIDS epidemic has the special quality of being an affliction of the "marginal" — of gays, who because of their sexual preferences, or of intravenous drug abusers, who because of their proverty and ignorance, are regarded as being "outside" the mainstream of American society. Although some fear that AIDS may soon massively enter this

---

[26] Resolutions to this effect have been passed in June 1986 by the 97th Annual Convention of the Central Conference of American Rabbis (a Reform organization) and, more recently, by the (Conservative) United Synagogue of America at its November 1987 Biennial Convention. At a meeting of its General Assembly (October 29-November 3, 1987), the Union of American Hebrew Congregations adopted a resolution "Confronting the AIDS Crisis" which advocated voluntary (as opposed to mandatory) testing programs for the AIDS virus, appropriate sex education, and active support in the spirit of *bikkur holim* for AIDS patients and their families.

"mainstream," the marginality of AIDS sufferers has tended to reduce this disease to an afterthought in the public consciousness and materially contributed to the slowness with which society initially responded to the crisis.

Jews and Jewish institutions have been as slow as others in this response. Removed from the plight of the inner cities, as inattentive to the presence of homosexuals in their midst as the Christian churches, Jews and Jewish organizations, with some notable exceptions, have not seen AIDS as a Jewish priority. Nevertheless, I would point out that Jews have always "specialized" in marginality. Not only have they frequently suffered persecution themselves as religious and moral outsiders, they have even sometimes been identified with the medically "misfit" and contagious. This theme can be found during the middle ages when Jews were accused and persecuted as fomenters of the plague or were charged with colluding with lepers in the effort to "contaminate" cities. More recently, we need only recall the ways in which the Nazis used the idea that Jews were bearers of genetic deformity or infectious disease (typhus, syphilis) as a pretext for mass exclusion and extermination.

The AIDS epidemic has subjected the gay community and, more recently, the inner-city poor to a similar process of exclusion. But the deepest resources of Jewish teaching issue a warning against any complicity with this way of thinking. In a recent discussion of the AIDS epidemic, Philip M. Kayal makes the interesting point that AIDS has not been just a negative experience for the gay community. As a terrible side effect of the suffering, says Kayal, AIDS has served to bring gay people together in new ways and has stimulated a newer more "inclusive and holistic way of relating and being in the world as a gay person." In this respect, and admittedly at frightful cost, Kayal believes that AIDS has stimulated an "incipient ethnogenesis" in the gay community.[27]

In the midst of this crisis, Jews should remember, and should try to share with others who look to their tradition for inspiration, the lesson that their experience as a people bears important similarities to these contemporary marginal groups. Jews also share an "ethnogenesis in suffering." If the Jewish people have endured to this day, it is because they consistently sought to learn from

---

[27] " 'Morals,' Medicine, and the AIDS Epidemic," *Journal of Religion and Health*, Vol. 24, No. 3, Fall 1985, 236.

suffering and have struggled to respond to it with realism and compassion. It is true that, where AIDS is concerned, most Jews are now part of mainstream culture. But they cannot forget their own long experience of marginality. Jews' fidelity to their tradition requires them to bring to this crisis the same combination of realism and compassion that marked their response to illness in the past.

Dr. Green is John Phillips Professor of Religion at Dartmouth College.

PRINCETON THEOLOGICAL SEMINARY
1988 SUMMER SCHOOL and
BIBLICAL LANGUAGE PROGRAM

June 6—July 29
Biblical Hebrew, Princeton Theological Seminary staff; **New Testament Greek**, Princeton Theological Seminary staff.

June 6—24
Jesus Within Judaism, James H. Charlesworth; **An Introduction to the Orthodox Tradition**, Paul Rorem; **Latin American Liberation Theology**, Daniel L. Migliore; **Ministry with Youth**, Freda A. Gardner; **Understanding Church Growth and Decline**, John R. Hendrick

June 27—July 15
Old Testament Theologies of War and Peace, Ben C. Ollenburger; **Creeds and Confessions, Canons and Decrees in Christian Theology from 1500 to 1650**, Edward A. Dowey, Jr.; **Vital Parish Education**, D. Campbell Wyckoff; **Preaching on Special Occasions**, Wade P. Huie, Jr.; **The Congregation as a Complex Organization**, Geddes W. Hanson; **Pastoral Care and the Life Cycle**, Donald E. Capps

July 18—August 5
The Interpretation of Paul's Letter to the Philippians, Steven J. Kraftchick; **Paul**

Tillich: Theologian of the Boundaries, Mark Kline Taylor; **Preacher and Poet Dialogue**, Christine M. Smith; **Teaching in the Church**, Donald Griggs; **Systems of Pastoral Marriage and Family Counseling,** Brian Childs; **Skills for the Resolution of Congregational Corporate Pain** and **Lab II—Developing Leaders for Lab I** in **Calling and Caring Ministries**, John S. and Joyce Savage

August 1—5
(followed by a month of independent study)
Foundations of Spirituality, Diogenes Allen; **Shattering Images: the Christian Dialogue with Buddhism**, Donald K. Swearer

Princeton Theological Seminary admits qualified students without regard to race, color, national or ethnic origin, disability or sex.

For full information write to
Summer School Office
Princeton Theological Seminary
108 Stockton Street, Princeton NJ 08540
or phone (609) 921-8252.

A SHARED PRAXIS APPROACH

James L. Street

Milligan College
Milligan College, TN 37682

If the church is to play a significant role in both ministering to the needs of AIDS victims and their families as well as ameliorating the hysteria and violence that appear to accompany the arrival of the AIDS virus in some communities, religious educators must be concerned not only with the effective diffusion of scientific information regarding the AIDS crisis but also with facilitating both helpful affective response and praxis.

The purpose of this article is to develop a particular educational philosophy for Christian religious education as it touches the AIDS crisis. This philosophy is grounded in Thomas Groome's "shared Christian praxis" model and is directed toward religious educators in church settings, although it could be generalized to other settings as well.[1]

Shared Christian Praxis

Groome describes Christian religious education by shared praxis as ". . . a group of Christians sharing in dialogue their critical reflection on present action in light of the Christian Story and its Vision toward the end of lived Christian faith."[2] He identifies five components of that approach:

> (1) Present Action — By present action Groome means that action that gives expression to the self. Therefore present action entails all that is done by oneself in the historical present. That present incorporates both the "present of things past and the present of things future."[3]

[1] Groome, Thomas, *Christian Religious Education: Sharing our Story and Vision* (New York: Harper and Row, 1980).

[2] Ibid., p. 184.

[3] Ibid., p. 185.

(2) Critical Reflection — Groome describes critical reflection as ". . . an activity in which one calls upon critical reason to evaluate the present, critical memory to uncover the past in the present and creative imagination to envision the future in the present." Critical reflection must begin with the self ". . . since action arises from the self."[4] In taking this perspective, Groome does not allow for the easy separation of self from the activity of the self but sees such activity as the inextricable expression of the self. Furthermore, such self-reflection takes into account the entire cultural mileu that gives rise to self-identity.

(3) Dialogue — Dialogue in the shared praxis approach entails inter-subjectivity. Each person in the educational setting brings to the shared moment his or her own past, present, and vision of the future. Such dialogue is more than mere "group discussion," which objectifies a particular subject domain. Instead, it seeks to wed heads to hearts in mutual sharing.[5]

(4) Story — The "story" under which participants in dialogue share and reflect is the Christian Story, which Groome describes as ". . . the whole faith tradition of our people however that is expressed or embodied."[6] Such a story is more than a narrative among narratives. Instead it ought to be understood in the way that Fowler uses the phrase "master story," which is that overarchmg, transcendent story under and within which each individual personal story is lived out in the life of faith.[7]

(5) Vision — Vision is the ". . . lived response which the Christian Story invites and . . . the promise which God makes in (the) Story."[8] Here Groome does not intend an apocalyptic, utopian vision of the "sweet by and by." Instead he intends that the Vision be lived out in the life of the Christian community. The Christian is called to help "unfold the Vision, rather than merely repeat the past."[9]

Having described the components of Groome's "shared praxis approach" to religious education, it is important to consider how such an approach can be utilized in helping the church understand its role with regard to the issue of public involvement and how the church can educate itself to deal justly and compassionately with the AIDS crisis. This will be accomplished by considering each facet of Groome's praxis model as it specifically touches the AIDS issue. While the approach delineated below is only illustrative, it does offer some guidance as to how his model may be "fleshed out" with regard to this particularly crucial concern.

---

[4] Ibid., p. 185.

[5] Ibid., p. 188.

[6] Ibid., p. 192.

[7] Fowler, James, *Stages of Faith: The Psychology of Human Development and the Quest for Meaning* (New York: Harper and Row, 1981), p. 277.

[8] Groome, p. 193.

[9] Ibid., p. 194.

Present Action

A significant portion of the shared praxis approach is the focus upon present action. Reflection centers upon one's ". . . present active engagement in the world as a Christian."[10] Such action embodies one's personal comprehension and vision of the Christian Story. However, although that expression is partially personal, it is also shared in the context of dialogue within a particular community of faith. Therefore, present action is self-expression as sponsored, encouraged, and constrained by a community of persons who share the Christian Story and Vision. However, several issues attach to the idea of present action.

First, one must recognize that there is no such thing as "nonbehavior."[11] Given the present level of understanding of the AIDS virus as something "objectified and out there," it is entirely possible that in many contexts no positive action is forthcoming. Yet inactivity is behavior. Persons engaged in shared praxis education around the issue of AIDS must be encouraged to reflect upon what they are doing in a situation where "doing" implies both action and inaction. In so doing, they should be led to reflect upon all possible motivations for both action and inaction. Action, inaction, supportiveness, apathy, compassion, and neglect are all expressions of the perception of the Story and the Vision. Action will not rise higher than either the individual's or the congregation's understanding of the Story and the Vision.

The second issue connected to the notion of "present action," therefore, has to do with congregational constraints on action. The religious educator deals not only with individuals but individuals-in-relationship. Fowler has recently suggested that there is possibly something that could be called the congregational "modal level of development," which he defines as ". . . the average expectable level of development for adults."[12] Religious educators who are interested in shared praxis education must take into account such "modal levels of development," especially with regard to discussion of the AIDS virus. For example, in some con-

---

[10] Ibid., p. 184.

[11] Watzlawick, Paul, Bavelas, Janet B., and Jackson, Don D. *Pragmatics of Human Communication* (New York: W. W. Norton and Co., 1967).

[12] Fowler, James, *Faith Development and Pastoral Care* (Philadelphia: Fortress Press, 1987), p. 81.

servative communities, social action is not seen to be a part of Christian vocation. That will be true especially when such social action may lead congregational members to engage others (especially outsiders) who have what is perceived to be a life-threatening, contagious disease.

Critical Reflection

Piaget wrote, "Intelligence organizes the world by organizing itself."[13] His point was that the knower is not merely a passive observer of concrete facts, which somehow fall into his or her consciousness. Piaget saw the human as an active knower who selects and transforms the world through the processes of attention, perception, and thought, all of which he considered to be action grounded in biological growth and experience.

This same sort of viewpoint is implied in the praxis approach to education. The task of the student is not only to see what there is to see but to delve into such questions as why at this or that particular moment he or she attends to this or that particular issue. As Groome writes, ". . . while critical reason begins by noticing the obvious in the present, it must delve below the obvious . . . to discover the interest in the present action, critique the ideology that maintains it, and recognize the assumptions upon which it is based."[14]

The praxis approach invites the participant to begin the slow and anxiety-provoking process of uncovering and questioning much of the tacit knowledge that underlies his or her assumptions as to the nature of reality. The participant questions that which is ordinarily taken for granted.

As it touches the AIDS question such a process entails asking oneself and being asked startling questions as to the criteria of judgments one employs in distinguishing oneself from the rest of the world, especially as that world is perceived as "other." In the process of dialogue, one seeks to ascertain one's deepest existential concerns as well as one's personal history insofar as that history has helped to call into being the person that one is. Further, insofar as language functions to define a person's experiential reality, the

---

[13] Quoted in Von Glaserfeld, Ernst, "An Introduction to Radical Constructivism," in Paul Waltzlawick (ed.) *The Invented Reality* (New York: W. W. Norton and Co., 1984), p. 24.

[14] Groome, p. 185.

careful analysis of words and phrases employed by participants opens up avenues into previously unexplored terrains.[15]

Specifically one struggles with personal views of the AIDS issue but also with cultural issues related to moral perspectives and indeed "hang-ups" regarding sexual practice, the poor, race, and class. Such an approach would not be only cognitive but affective as well. As Groome wrote, ". . . (in praxis) critical reflection is an affair of both the heart and the head . . . when we critically reflect on present action, it is primarily our own selves we come to know, and we cannot know ourselves dispassionately. Head and heart are fused inevitably in self-knowledge."[16]

Dialogue

In a praxis approach to religious education, the dialogue that occurs between participants is not only a particular means to interpersonal discovery, it is also isomorphic to religious engagement with the world. This point has been well developed by Paulo Friere, who has written at length about the dangers of treating educational method as neutral to content.[17] Educational method can serve an alienating function if content about humans is devoid of contact with humans.

In other words, to consider only persons with AIDS, or families with members with AIDS, or health care professionals who work with persons with AIDS "in the abstract" serves the process of dehumanization. This process distances the subject area from those who seek to "dialogue" about it. The process of educational dialogue, which occurs in the context of the religion classroom, should model for the student the kind of engagement required if persons who are daily touched by the illness in one form or another are to be aided, indeed humanized. Although statistical kinds of information help the student to gain an overview of the problem, statistics are not persons. Praxis education above all seeks to humanize.[18] To think or even to dialogue about humans without ever actually engaging humans, whatever the issue, alienates and dehumanizes.

---

[15] cf. Watzlawick et al., *Pragmatics of Human Communication*, op. cit. Also see his book entitled *How Real is Real?* (New York: Vintage Books, 1976).

[16] Groome, p. 188.

[17] Freire, Paulo, "Education, Liberation and the Church," in *Religious Education*, 79, 4, Fall, 1984.

[18] Ibid. p. 532.

The Story

Because of the nature of the crisis and the potential for large scale devastation, the AIDS crisis will continue to force a re-thinking of the central facets of the Christian Story. In order to illustrate the interplay between the learner and the Story, only two facets will be considered: (1) the nature of God as revealed in Jesus and (2) the nature and the purpose of the church.

Perhaps a story will more efficiently demonstrate how the AIDS crisis can force a re-thinking of Christology. While I was preparing this manuscript, I happened to mention to a class of college students a sermon I had recently preached called, "AIDS: A Test for the Church." The students asked what had been said.

The sermon utilized the story in Luke in which Jesus healed a man "covered with leprosy" by reaching out and touching him. The point of the sermon was to illustrate the compassion and freedom of Jesus in his encounter with the physically ill and stigmatized.

One student in the class remarked that the text was not appropriate for the topic. I expected him to say that AIDS was not leprosy and that the comparisons may not have been justified, which would have been a legitimate point. However, that was not his objection at all. He claimed it was illegitimate to utilize Jesus as a symbol of encounter with "the diseased" because ". . . as the Son of God Jesus could not have become ill with the disease and even if he had he could have healed himself."

Although such a response appears naive from the standpoint of someone trained in theology and logic, it does illustrate some vitally important issues.

First, it illustrates the tacit dimension of theological knowledge. The student in question had undoubtedly never given much thought to the question of the humanity of Jesus and what that implies. Second, and even more important, is the relationship this tacit knowledge of the determinative image of Jesus bears to that particular student's perception of his own responsibility in the face of the crisis. For him, giving Jesus a "divine edge" automatically would exclude any sort of direct response himself, a "mere human." Third, the incident demonstrates the dynamic interplay that exists between the demands of everyday social life and the dominant images that occupy a person's mind.[19]

---

[19] Fowler, *Stages of Faith.*

The point is that it would be misguided for the religious educator to concern himself or herself with confining the discussion of
the AIDS virus to known scientific fact only or with narrowly defined objectives such as "keeping the kids in the youth group from
catching it." The AIDS crisis touches every dominant symbol of
Christian faith and therefore serves as a catalyst in the restructur-
ing of the whole of theological knowing, that is, the Story.

The AIDS crisis will also touch that facet of the Christian Story
having to do with the nature and purpose of the Church. For example, it will provoke discussion as to the private versus public
nature of the church.

Fowler has delineated four characteristics of "the public
church": (1) a deep and particular commitment to God's self-
revelation in Jesus Christ; (2) a prepared willingness to pursue
mission and ministry in a pluralistic society; (3) a concern for intimacy within the community counter-balanced by care about the
impersonal and structural domains of public life; and (4) a non-
defensive willingness to engage with the complexities and ambiguities of thought in this age of ideological pluralism.[20]

Although Fowler's description of the "private church" is not as
clearly defined as his description of the "public church," he does
suggest at least three characteristics of such a church: (1) the expectation that the real satisfactions and fulfillments of life will
come from interpersonal relations; (2) that the members of such
churches are drawn and restrict themselves to circles of similar,
like-minded others; and (3) that work and interaction in public
life are merely roles that are played ". . . in order to secure, earn,
and enjoy life in the private sphere."[21]

Some specific issues that emerge out of the church's decision
as to its degree of "publicness" or "privateness" include how those
particular churches address (1) issues of community involvement
(especially as such involvement touches the poor, the homeless,
the homosexual and the different ethnic groups); (2) human sexual practice and sex education; (3) the plurality of ideologies,
values, and practices which are prevalent in our society; (4)
ecumenicity (i.e. the degree of willingness to network with both
religious and secular organizations in concerted educational, service, and advocacy efforts); (5) the relationship of church (i.e.

---

[20] Fowler, *Faith Development and Pastoral Care*, p. 24.
[21] Ibid. p. 23.

doctrine and dogma) to science; and (6) both the postoral and prophetic dimensions of ministry.

How particular churches respond to the AIDS crisis will in large part reflect the kinds of decisions that are made with regard to their level of "publicness." Again, how religious educators approach the topic will certainly affect a church's decisions. It would seem that if a church elects to be a "private church" in the face of compelling needs, then that church will have little to offer except the promise of personal salvation as narrowly and pietistically defined. This may pose a particularly significant challenge to churches with a conservative or fundamentalist orientation. It is incumbent upon religious educators to develop the means and the opportunities for "shared Christian praxis" around the issue of AIDS so that the churches that benefit from their labors will be in the position to serve rather than to shirk from active public involvement.

Vision

Vision may be understood as the individual-in-community's and the community's participation in establishing the presence of the coming Kingdom. In light of the Christian Story, God's activity in human history calls for continued and renewed response. As Groome writes, "We must appropriate the Story critically within the present experience, reclaim it, add to it with our own creative word and in that sense 'change' it."[22]

However, the Vision always calls into question one's present praxis.[23] This is true because no matter what is being done in the name of the Vision, it is always incomplete and distorted. Therefore, the Vision both critiques and calls. It critiques what is present and calls forth what is not yet but can be.

With regard to the AIDS problem, the Vision beckons participants to imagine what is possible in the present and in the future. Specifically, the educator should facilitate critical reflection and dialogue upon present action with regard to the AIDS issue in light of the evocative power of the Story and the Vision. What this means, of course, is that participants will have to reflect upon issues of justice and compassion. Further, they will have to think through the role of the church with regard to advocacy before governmental agencies at the local, state, and federal levels.

[22] Groome, p. 194.
[23] Ibid. p. 197.

However, it is not only imperative that participants think critically and reflect upon the shape of ministry regarding AIDS at that very broad, structural level; they will also have to think in terms of their personal response to the AIDS carrier who sits down or kneels to share the common cup in worship, and their parental response when their child must sit next to another child with AIDS in the classroom at the local public school. Such decisions will affect praxis at the level of advocacy before local school boards and school officials. Before the issues of worship are settled, there could be mass exits in congregations of people too frightened to risk fellowship with the dying.

Summary

Religious educators must decide if they wish to broach the AIDS topic in the context of the church. While many will undoubtedly wish to take a stand, the implicit suggestion of this article is that before that is done, the religious educator must count the cost.

People are terribly frightened by the AIDS virus. Although fear must be overcome, it should also be understood and compassionately and patiently worked through. AIDS reminds people of the limitations of scientific know-how. It confronts people in a way that demands response unlike any other social issue. The disease touches people in ways that question existential security and personal taste and history.

Religious educators should work through these issues themselves before they expect others to do likewise. Modeling appropriate praxis does most to teach appropriate praxis.

Religious educators should be sensitive to the isssue of "congregational presence," which Fowler defines as ". . . the typical patterns of interest and interpretation (which can be anticipated) in congregations."[24] Often theologically trained religious educators find themselves in congregations where critical reflection and social action are not valued. In those cases, religious educators will have to develop empathic means by which to enter the world of those who hold belief more implicitly and conventionally and who value the maintenance of interpersonal relationships more highly than the "threats" imposed by critical thinking on significant social praxis.

Dr. Street is associate professor of psychology at Milligan College.

---

[24] Fowler, *Faith Development and Pastoral Care*, p. 82.

GOD'S PUNISHMENT FOR SIN?

Walter E. Wiest

Pittsburgh Theological Seminary
Pittsburgh, Pennsylvania 15228

Few problems in today's world have raised more varied and extensive ethical questions than the AIDS epidemic. The aim of this essay is to deal primarily with the issue of moral blame.

Should we look upon AIDS as punishment for immorality in the sense in which we punish children for misbehavior or criminals for breaking the law? I shall give reasons for holding that such a view is ethically and theologically unsound and can have unfortunate consequences for the ways we respond to the AIDS epidemic. At the same time, morally responsible acts do play a leading part in the transmission of the disease, and this fact complicates the ethics of the situation. We need to sort out the ethical and the biomedical considerations, to see their proper distinctions and connections. Failure to do so will result in mistakes both in ethical judgment and quite possibly in decisions about what practical measures should be taken to meet the threat which now confronts us.

Infection can occur through contacts that lay no moral blame on the victim. Babies can be infected by their mothers. A wife or husband can be infected by a spouse. There are special risks for medical personnel who might be exposed to the blood of patients, though these risks can apparently be minimized by certain protective procedures. Such persons as police and firefighters could be exposed through contact with injured persons. AIDS has been contracted through blood transfusions. All this points to the basically biological character of AIDS and its epidemic potentialities.

It is still true, however, that in the overwhelming majority of cases, infected persons have acquired the disease through sexual contacts (especially anal sex practices) and intravenous drug-taking (sharing the needle). Our only reasonably sure protection is to abstain from intravenous drugs and promiscuous sex. This advice is sound whether we view such acts as morally right or morally wrong. The basis of the advice is biomedical, not moral.

From an ethical viewpoint, the acts in question have been weighed and judged wrong (or right, as the case may be) for ethical reasons. We did not have to wait for the AIDS epidemic in order to make these judgments. Surely most of us would agree that there is a more positive moral motivation for doing what is right than the negative motivation of being punished with a fatal disease. Over the centuries, countless numbers of people have refrained from promiscuous sex because they thought it to be immoral. If they indulged, they did so with guilty consciences. On the other hand, those who today believe such behavior acceptable do not seem to have changed their minds because of AIDS. As indicated in various articles recently, they seem rather to see AIDS as an unfortunate, in some sense even "unfair," restriction on their "right" to sexual freedom.

For Christians, especially, the distinction between medical and ethical perspectives is pertinent. Christian attitudes toward various kinds of sexual behavior have been based upon ethical principles formulated long before AIDS appeared. Although it is true that today there is less agreement among Christians in their attitudes toward such issues, there are few indeed who defend promiscuity, whether heterosexual or homosexual.

Much of the confusion about AIDS and morality is due to the failure to distinguish between two levels of responsibility. This is true both of those who see AIDS as punishment and of those who want to defend AIDS victims as free of moral blame. An example of the latter is found in a statement made by James Hurley, a victim of AIDS, reported in a recent issue of *Newsweek*:

> I got AIDS in a sexually promiscuous time, in the late 70's in New York. . . . We didn't know what was out there . . . so I caught AIDS out of ignorance. . . . It galls me when I hear one of those reporters mention that the babies who contract AIDS through their mothers are the *innocent* victims of AIDS, as though the rest of us are *guilty* victims. There's no such thing as an innocent or guilty victim of AIDS. Either you have AIDS or you don't have AIDS. It doesn't make any difference how it was contracted. To have it is to have a disease that will end your life.[1]

---

[1] *Newsweek*, August 10, 1987, p. 38.

I have the greatest sympathy for Mr. Hurley as I have for all victims of AIDS. Still, I have problems with his statement:

1. Babies who contract AIDS through their mothers are clearly innocent victims in any sense.

2. Adults who contracted AIDS before they had a chance to know anything about the disease are not to be blamed in one sense; that is, they could not have been expected to protect themselves against a disease about which they knew nothing. What Hurley's statement does not seem to recognize is that an adult has a responsibility once the disease is identified and its means of transmission known. To say that "there is no such thing as an innocent or guilty victim of AIDS" is to ignore this difference between infants and adults, and between adults who are informed and those who are not.

3. Once a person has AIDS, it is true that there is an important sense in which "it doesn't make any difference how it was contracted." Certainly this is true in a medical sense. The medical causes and consequences are the same for all, and so is the moral responsibility of medical professionals to treat and extend care. On these matters, medical ethics and Christian ethics are in agreement. But these truths need to be distinguished from other considerations about the actions through which the disease may have been contracted in the first place. Persons who have become ill through their own ill-advised behavior have a responsibility for their plight, which is not shared by others who have become ill through no detectable fault of their own.

4. Perhaps the most serious question is raised by the statement, "I got AIDS in a sexually promiscuous time, in the late '70's in New York," when this statement is placed in the context of a general contention that all AIDS victims are "innocent." Hurley bases his contention mainly on the fact that the danger of AIDS was not known at the time, a point we have already accepted. But does he also mean that sexual promiscuity is "innocent" in itself, that apart from AIDS it is quite acceptable behavior? Does he mean that it was acceptable because of the trend of the time? Either implication would raise serious ethical questions.

Hurely has a right to his own moral views. The important thing is to see that there is another kind of responsibility that must be considered. Quite apart from knowledge of disease and its consequences, sexual behavior is subject to ethical evaluation. Two sorts of responsibility must be distinguished. A person's behavior can be "cleared" in one respect while still being open to ethical judgment in the other.

It seems that defenders of the innocence of AIDS victims can sometimes make the same mistake, in reverse, as those who see AIDS as a punishment for immorality. Both can confuse moral judgments with judgments about physical causes and consequences. One says, "If you contract AIDS, it is because you have acted immorally." The other says, "If you contract AIDS, it is for purely physical reasons, not moral ones. Therefore, you are morally innocent." The source of the confusion is that both views connect the moral and the physical dimensions too directly and simplistically. They leave out the distinction between the responsibility we have for determining what is right or wrong on purely moral grounds and the more practical and prudential responsibility we have for avoiding actions that can expose us to disease. In fact, we might indulge in promiscuous sexual behavior and still avoid AIDS through an astute or lucky choice of sexual partners. We might also contract AIDS through ignorance, and therefore in one sense innocently, while at the same time our promiscuous sexual activity would still be open to ethical criticism.

When we move on to theological implications, we find ourselves confronting the age-old question of theodicy. If God created the world and continues to govern it, but the world operates unjustly, is God then unjust? For our purpose, the question is specifically whether there is any evidence of a relationship between human moral conduct and health or sickness. Is there any indication that disese afflicts the unrighteous rather than, or even more than, the righteous? Is AIDS a punishment of God upon the unrighteous?

Those who answer "yes" to the latter question may well be lumping two ideas together. One of them might be called a doctrine of *general* providence: the belief that there is a general ordering of the world that connects the moral with the physical so that good people prosper while evil people are penalized. The other is a doctrine of *special* providence: the belief that God intervenes in particular instances in order to reward the virtuous and punish evildoers. In the Old Testament, this belief occurs in the context of covenant. God establishes a covenant with a people. The covenant includes laws to govern the people's conduct. If they obey the laws, they are rewarded. If not, they are punished. The early American Puritans believed they had such a covenant with God, interpreting their experiences in this light. If things went badly for them, they assembled in worship to make confession of whatever sins they may have committed and to ask God's forgiveness. If things went well, they assembled to thank God for rewarding them for whatever they had done right. Some conservative American Protestants still tend to see their nation this way and consequently tend to interpret AIDS as divine punishment.

From the standpoint of the facts of experience, such views seem unsupportable. We know that "bad things happen to good people." Individuals who die from cancer or heart disease, or who suffer through much of their lives from severe arthritis, or are born with painful and incapacitating physical ailments, are not observably less virtuous than others who enjoy robust health through most of their long lives. If we give up the concept of general providence, we might still believe that God intervenes in particular situations and that God has inflicted AIDS as punishment for specific ethical offenses. But why, then, has God failed to decree such punishment for oppressing the poor, or abusing wives and children? Why are murderers not so obviously afflicted? Where is the justice in it all?

Actually, such thinking is rejected in the book of Job. Job's uncomforting friends assume a causal relation between disease and immorality. If Job has boils, he must have sinned. Job denies this. In three rounds of debate, he proclaims his innocence and even offers an indictment of God for injustice. God is challenged to justify what has happened. Job receives an answer. The initial response comes in the voice from the whirlwind. Job has challenged the order of the world, but what does he know about the complexities of making and sustaining a world? He has not created. He was not present when this world was created. His wisdom is not adequate to the task. He is presumptuous.

John Hick has pursued the implications of this view in his book, *Evil and the God of Love*.[2] His main point is that the order of the world, which makes possible the good things we cherish, seems necessarily to involve the bad things we decry. The same order that affords us our existence and the things necessary to our life is the order that includes predators and prey. The order that makes possible the products of human creativity (artistic, scien-

---

[2] New York: Harper and Row, 1966.

tific, sociological, etc.) also makes possible diseases such as AIDS. Can we conceive of a world order better than this? The trouble is that we know of only one world order, the one we have. Are we really competent to project another and allegedly better one?

The other response is implicit but, I believe, just as unmistakable. At the beginning of the book, in the "prologue in heaven," Satan poses the most fundamental question. Does Job worship God because he prospers, or because he truly loves God? Would he still love and serve God if his prosperity were taken away? Through most of the book, Job actually accepts the thesis of his friends. If he has been righteous, he should prosper. His sufferings are unjust. The response that comes is not that he is less innocent than he supposes, though we might guess that this is so. Rather, it is that he has taken a too limited view of God and of the divine purposes. Human desires and satisfactions are not the be-all and end-all of creation. God has larger purposes, to which humans are expected to adjust.[3] God does not exist to serve humans but humans to serve God, and God is to be worshipped because he is God. We cannot expect God to arrange the world according to our notions. We should not serve God because we hope for reward or fear punishment.

Sobered by all this, Job says: "I know that you can do everything, that nothing you propose is impossible for you. . . . Indeed, I spoke without understanding of things beyond me, which I did not know. . . . I had heard you with my ears, but now I see you with my eyes; therefore, I recant and relent, being but dust and ashes." God then says to Eliphaz, one of Job's friends: "I am incensed at you and your two friends, for you have not spoken the truth about me as did my servant Job" (42.2-7). The friends' view is flatly rejected. There is no assumable connection between physical illness and sin, or material prosperity and virtue.

In the New Testament, the case is even clearer. The question of Job in the Old Testament, according to Reinhold Niebuhr, is thrown back to us as the answer in the New. Redemption is to come about through suffering. It is not sinners whose suffering is in view, but the suffering of the righteous. The moral standards

---

[3] James M. Gustafson, in *Ethics from a Theological Perspective* (University of Chicago Press, Vol. I, 1981, and Vol. II, 1984), has elaborated this theme impressively, showing its theological dimensions and its implications for Christian ethics.

and motivations of the Kingdom are in stark contrast to those of the human world we know. When this world is challenged, the regnant powers react oppressively. The call of the Kingdom puts all other considerations in the shade. It is of no moment whether the man born blind suffered because of his own or his parents' sins (John 9.1-12) or whether those upon whom the tower of Siloam fell were more sinful than others (Luke 13.1-5). In fact, the whole calculus of rewards and punishments is rejected or, rather, it is surpassed. We are all sinners. We all need to be forgiven and graciously redeemed and reconciled. If there is a relationship between righteousness/unrighteousness and suffering, it is found in the suffering we do for righteousness' sake.

The conclusion seems obvious. Although we still need to make distinctions between righteous and unrighteous behavior — sexual promiscuity is no more compatible with the morality of the Kingdom than is murder or the oppression of the powerless and the poor — we are not justified in using this moral judgment as the primary basis of our reaction to the victims of AIDS. Self-righteous condemnation is simply not a Christian attitude. Jesus' own way of caring about sufferers and of relating to them lovingly regardless of their sins points in a different direction. Without approving of immoral behavior, we are to acknowledge our common sinfulness and respond to sufferers with love and care. In this area especially, caring is the primary virtue, both in Christian and in medical ethics.

Those Christians who interpret AIDS as God's punishment for sin seem to welcome it as a God-sent confirmation and reinforcement of Christian morality. Why should we need such a confirmation? If any others were converted by it, would they be moved by anything other than self-interested fear of punishment? It is instructive to recall Jesus' response to those who demanded a "sign" from him, a divine signal of his authority and the authenticity of his message. If they had really understood his proclamation of the coming of the Kingdom and of the repentance and new life which response to it entailed, they would not have needed any other verification or motivation. Consequently, Jesus' reply was that they would get no sign except the sign of Jonah. G. B. Caird's interpretation of this somewhat cryptic reply seems right:

> Those who asked for a sign wanted some spectacular proof that Jesus was the emissary of God he claimed to be. He replied that the only proof of his credentials he was prepared to give was that which Jonah offered to the Ninevites; Jonah called them to repentance, and in his

words they recognized the authentic demand of God. The same demand was present in the preaching of Jesus, and those who were deaf to it were not likely to be convinced by any other form of authentication.[4]

Applied to the AIDS situation, this surely means that we do not need AIDS as a "sign" to confirm our sense of what is morally right or to motivate us to do the right as we see it. At least, we *should* not need such a sign.

———————

Dr. Wiest is professor emeritus of philosophy of religion at Pittsburgh Theological Seminary.

———————

[4] *St. Luke, Pelican Gospel Commentary* (Baltimore: Penguin Books, Ltd., 1963) on Luke 11.27-36, p. 156.

IMAGINATION AND FAITH DEVELOPMENT

David J. Loomis

Prescott, Arizona 86303

Imagination is the cognitive faculty that mediates a person's relationship with God. Two qualities that inhere in imaginative activity — first, its ability to integrate the mental, emotional, and motor-sensory dimensions of human existence, and, second, its openness to God's realm of pure possibility — enable imagination to facilitate and mediate the divine-human relationship.

Imagination's Integrative Function

Recent research in neurophysiology finds imaginal activity to be whole-brained, non-lateralized, equally distributed through the entire frontal cortex area, the area that is so directly involved with our reasoning capabilities.[1] Yet imaginative activity also shows strong connections with the limbic and hippocampal areas that control our emotional and motor activities.[2] Powerful dreams, dreams that cause physical and emotional arousal and also provide reason with clues of an illuminating character, attest to the integrative power of imagination. Such integration explains why religious symbols (like the cross or the holocaust) play such an important role in human existence. Not only do these symbols speak to the meaning or meaninglessness of life as a whole, they also involve the whole person with life as a whole.

Imagination's Realm of Pure Possibility

Imagination also is unique in its capacity to entertain a realm of pure possibility. Behind kinetic energy lies potential energy. Be-

---

[1] Ley, R. G., "Cerebral Laterality and Imagery," in *Imagery*, (A. Sheikh, Ed.) (New York: John Wiley & Sons, 1983), p. 255.

[2] Hart, L. A., *Human Brain and Human Learning* (New York: Langman Inc., 1983), p. 41.

hind the senses' realm of actuality and reason's realm of probability lies imagination's realm of possibility. Phenomenologist Edward S. Casey writes

> Of each imaginative presentation I experience, it could be said that in it *anything* was possible; no particular object or event had to appear there in the first place, or to appear there in any specific way. The latitude introduced by the factor of pure possibility brings with it a sense of endlessness — of open development, which is limited only by the particular content of a given presentation.[3]

Such freedom from reason's realm of probability and the body's realm of actuality allows imagination to enter fully into God's infinite realm of possibility. If the Old and New Testaments have definitive theological formula to offer human reason, it is to be found in the Old Testament's divine self-definition, "I will be what I will be" (Exodus 3:14) and in the New Testament's recurring theme, "With God all things are possible" (Mat. 19:26, Mark 10:27 and 14:36, Luke 1:37 and 19:26).

So crucial is imagination for entering and perceiving God's realm of pure possibility that Scripture, with few exceptions, addresses us imaginatively. We are told incredible story after incredible story. We are, in fact, being told God's story, which reaches out to grip our imaginations with its improbable happenings and baffling mysteries. Even when Scripture refers to God directly, it normally employs poetic metaphors — God is Spirit, Love, Lord, Light, Word, Shepherd, Father, Son, King — metaphors that effectively solicit an imaginative response in us and which thereby are able to arouse deep-seated feelings.

Scripture and Imagination

One contemporary theologian, David Harned, has concluded that Scripture's understanding of the divine-human relationship omits imagination, Scripture emphasizing the Word of God with the ear and not the eye, serving as the primary medium of revelation.[4]

No doubt the Bible invites people to attune their inner ear — their intuition and conscience — to God's still, small voice. But such attunement can be readily construed as a function of audi-

---

[3] Casey, E. S., *Imagining; A Phenomenological Study* (Bloomington, Ind.: Indiana University Press, 1979), p. 37.

[4] Harned, D. B., *Faith and Virtue* (Philadelphia, Pa.: Pilgrim Press, 1973), p. 13.

tory imagination. Imagination operates through every sensory modality (auditory, visual, olfactory, tactile, gustatory, and kinesthetic),[5] as well as beyond them in acts of linguistic and mathematical creativity. And the Bible does not conceive God's revelation as Word, but as Word made flesh, as Word incarnate in human history. Such a mystery is best perceived imaginatively.

Scripture attests to God's "signs and wonders," a phrase that occurs 13 times in the Old Testament and 16 in the New Testament, lending it a fair degree of credibility. To those without the imagination to perceive these signs and to wonder about these wonders, it is as if God were playing wedding music and no one was dancing, or funeral music and no one crying (Mat. 11:16; Luke 7:32). "Are your hearts hardened? Do you have eyes and fail to see, ears and fail to hear" (Mark 8:18)? Yet, to those with heartfelt imaginative capabilities, "Blessed are your eyes, for they see; and your ears for they hear" (Mat. 13:16).

The New Testament envisions such "ontological imagination" (William James' phrase) as now being restored, God's Spirit of truth releasing imagination from captivity to the strivings of human ego and libido. Both as a species and individually, God's Spirit is liberating humankind from that time when "God saw that the wickedness of man was great in the earth, and that every imagination of his heart was only evil continuously" (Gen. 6:05). What we perceive now as through veils — or as "through a glass darkly" — will someday be "face-to-face" (I Cor. 13:12). Reason will then confirm what imagination now dimly perceives through its intimations both of God and of immortality.

> But whenever anyone turns to the Lord, the veil is taken away. . . .
> And we who, with unveiled faces, all reflect the Lord's glory, are being transformed into his likeness with every-increasing glory, which comes from the Lord, who is the Spirit (II Cor. 3:16-18).

That this process of transformation (faith development) involves a steadily increasing imaginative capacity is witnessed to quite beautifully by Mark's story of the healing of the blind man at Bethsaida. First the blind man sees "men as trees, walking." Then, touched "again upon his eyes" and told to "look up," his sight improves, until he "saw every man clearly" (Mark 8:22-25).

Jesus repeatedly conveys the need for imaginative insight if

---

[5] Achterberg, J., *Imagery and Healing* (Boston: Shambhala Press, 1985), p. 3.

his disciples are to perceive God. When his disciples wonder why
he "always" speaks "in parables," he says

> . . . because they seeing, see not; and hearing, they hear not, neither
> do they understand (Mat. 13:13).

Only those whose hearts have been touched by God's spirit of
truth are free to understand, to perceive, however dimly, the
height and depth and glory of God's eternal kingdom of possibility.

> The light of the body is the eye; if therefore your eye be healthy, your
> whole body shall be full of light. But if your eye be evil, your whole
> body shall be darkness (Mat. 6:20).

Jesus' closing words to his disciples are, "You must be ready!"
Surrounding this imperative are two final references to the need
for imaginative insight. "Watch therefore, for you know not the
hour when your Lord will come," and "Watch therefore, for you
know neither the day nor the hour when the Son of man will be
coming" (Mat. 24:14 and 25:13). In Luke's Gospel, being ready
means to look within, imaginatively, not outwardly to history, for
insight concerning the Lord's coming (Luke 17:20).

The Old Testament concludes with the prophets, those with
insight, the "seers." The New Testament concludes with the Book
of Revelation, writing that begs for imaginative interpretation.
Through Scripture, God nurtures the life of imagination, even as
God's spirit of truth has freed human imagination from the grip of
sin to be re-planted in God's eternal kingdom of possibility.

> And in the last days it shall be, God declares, that I will pour out my
> Spirit upon all flesh, and your sons and your daughters shall be seers,
> and your young men shall see visions, and your old men shall dream
> dreams (Acts 2:17).

Depth Psychology, Imagination, and Religious Faith

Without question, depth psychology has been responsible for raising to contemporary Western consciousness the revelatory role of
imaginative activity. To be sure, Origen loved to interpret Scripture allegorically. The monastic movement produced people
versed in the arts of visual meditation. The Romantic period saw
Coleridge proclaim the imagination to be nothing less than "a
repetition in the finite mind of the eternal, infinite I AM."[6] And

---

[6] Coleridge, S. T., *Bibliographia Literaria, Vol. 1* (Oxford: Clarendon Press, 1908),
p. 16.

Kierkegaard found in imagination the gracious means by which reason and affect could be brought into both "equilibrium" and "simultaneity" within the life of faith.[7] But only in the last three decades have theologians assumed imagination to be deeply implicated in God's revelatory activity, an assumption growing out of depth psychology's discovery that religious faith was grounded in imaginative activity.

Freud must be credited with being the first psychodynamic thinker to connect imagination directly with faith. He concluded that ". . . religious ideas, which are given us as teachings, are not percipitates of experience or end results of thinking; they are illusions, fulfillments of the oldest, strangest, and most urgent wishes of mankind."[8]

Seventy years later, standing squarely within the Freudian school, R. H. Hook looked at the same data and reversed Freud's negative assessment of faith's connection with wishful thinking. Hook concluded that imagination could be trusted to create myths and symbols that were authentic "instinctual" representations of human reality, able to "mediate between reality and the mind's apprehension of reality."[9] Without spiritual imaginings, "human behaviour would be segmental and impoverished, man unable to make full contact with reality, and therefore with himself."[10]

Jung was the first psychodynamic thinker to suggest that it was reality-prone imagination (insight — "einbildungskraft"), not pleasure-oriented imagination (fantasy — "phantasia"), that was more closely associated with spiritual growth and discovery. Jung became aware of a depth dimension of human consciousness that lay beyond the personal unconscious so dear to Freudian analysis. He named this deeper zone the "collective unconscious" and identified the dawn of mature religious faith with any person becoming more open to "imaginative representations that mediate between the universal collective unconscious and the free will of the individual ego."[11]

---

[7] Kierkegaard, S., *Concluding Unscientific Postscript* (Princeton, NJ: Princeton University Press, 1941), p. 311.

[8] Freud, S., *The Future of an Illusion* (London: Routledge Press, 1917), p. 30.

[9] Hook, R. H., "Fantasy and Symbol; a psychological point of view" in *Fantasy and Symbol* (R. H. Hook, Ed.) (New York: Academia Press, 1979), p. 277.

[10] Ibid., p. 9.

[11] Jung, C. G., *The Symbolic Life* (Princeton: Princeton University Press, 1956), p. 267.

Theology, Imagination, and Religious Faith

In the mid-1950s, theologians such as Paul Tillich, H. Richard Niebuhr, and Dorothy Emmet began to focus attention on the contribution of imagination to the life of faith. Tillich's work clearly reflects Jung's influence. For Tillich, religious beliefs "cannot be produced intentionally."

> They grow out of the collective unconscious and cannot function without being accepted by the unconscious dimension of our being. Symbols of faith cannot be replaced by other symbols, such as artistic ones, and they cannot be removed by scientific criticism. They have a genuine standing in the human mind, just as science and art have.[12]

Tillich glimpsed that divine revelation ultimately involves human imagination entering God's realm of "impossible possibility."

Just two years earlier, H. Richard Niebuhr had made the first twentieth-century theological statement of the intimate connection between imagination and revelation.

> (The Church) cannot make a choice between reason and imagination, but only between reasoning on the basis of adequate images and thinking with the aid of evil imaginations. . . . By revelation in our history, then, we mean that special occasion which provides us with an image by means of which all the occasions of personal and common life become intelligible.[13]

It fell to Dorothy Emmet to tackle the thorny issue of the actual "reality" of all such revelatory imaginings.

> Man's images of the transcendent are, therefore, from the first not merely literal . . . they are attempts to express a unique relationship. But to say this raises a question rather than answers it. Is there in fact some real relationship to be so expressed?[14]

She answers her question with this affirmation: that religious faith is akin in its intuitive judgments of reality to other such commonplace intuitive judgments as that someone's moral character is "sound," or that a particular work of art is "convincing." Yet she finds a vital difference between religious intuitions of divine reality and all other such intuitive judgments:

> A poem may carry conviction as the reconstruction of a way of responding to life. We can give it "real assent" . . . without also com-

---

[12] Tillich, P., *Dynamics of Faith* (New York: Harper & Row, 1957), p. 43.

[13] Niebuhr, H. R., *The Meaning of Revelation* (New York: MacMillan, 1953), p. 108-109.

[14] Emmet, D. M., *The Nature of Metaphysical Thinking* (New York: St. Martin's Press, 1957), p. 415.

mitting ourselves to accepting its "philosophy of life" when we are not
reading the poem. . . . we can observe "psychic distance" from the
poem. But the religious total assertion is a conscious responsive relation
in which our whole nature is somehow committed . . . having to do
with what concerns us most deeply.[15]

For Emmet, all such intuitive judgments occur "below the level
of conscious reasoning . . . akin to the experience of creative inspiration."[16] Being consciously developed, then tested and re-
tested in terms of their reliability, they can be trusted to express
far more of reality than they do of fantasy.

Prominent English Catholic literary critic, John Coulson, has
written along similar lines, concluding that religious faith to be
believed must "first be credible to imagination."

. . . what we hold in faith is most frequently expressed in metaphor,
symbol, and story, and, as such, prior to and as a condition of its verification, it requires imaginative assent comparable to that given to
poems and novels.[17]

For Coulson, religious symbols cannot be arbitrary and hope to
remain around for centuries. They must do far more than great
poems and novels do. Not only must they suspend disbelief, they
must go further, predisposing people to believe in what they sig-
nify. Coulson concludes that religious faith begins in what "imagination has realized," then moves through belief toward understanding.

. . . the theologian is wise if he (sic) seeks renewal of belief where
poetry and religion modulate into each other. If he is to make a real
assent to the objects of faith, the theologian must use his imagination,
which means undertaking the intolerable wrestle with meaning, since
what he seeks lies 'hid in language.' He seeks imaginative assents which
are convertible into certitudes.[18]

Coulson's theo-poetic theme can also be located in the recent
work of Harvey Cox:

Theologians should be transmuting old symbols, exploring alternative
metaphors, juxtaposing unlikely concepts, playing with new and improbable images of man and of woman, God and world, earth and
sky. . . . The "ology" part of "theology" comes from the Greek logos

---

[15] Ibid., p. 444.

[16] Ibid., p. 143-144.

[17] Coulson, J., *Religion and Imagination* (Oxford: Clarendon Press, 1981), p. ii.

[18] Ibid., p. 168.

("word," "meaning," "significance"). To banish the imaginative side of
life to the il-logical, in-significant, or meaningless is to accept a crip-
pling restriction on what counts as meaning.[19]

If God's truth be stranger than fiction, as Scripture would suggest
that it surely must be, the word of modern theology would seem
to be that we who seek to discern and share that truth would do
well to seek it imaginatively.

Testing this Hypothesis

At a recent ecumenical conference on faith development in Stony
Brook, New York, I asked the conferees how many could give a
clear "Yes" or "No" to this statement: "Imagination is important to
faith formation." Of 28 participants, ten answered "Yes," 12 "No,"
and the rest were uncertain — rather clearly a hung jury.

If I had asked the same group to respond to the statements:
"Experiences of God's living presence are important to faith formation," or "Growing up in a devout home full of loving faith is
important to faith formation," or "Seeing oneself as a full-time
servant of God is important to faith formation," I am sure I would
have received a higher percentage of affirmative replies.

Beyond this issue of whether imagination contributes to faith
development lay the question as to the actual magnitude of any
such contribution (relative to other factors, such as mystical experience, which may also contribute to faith development).

To help answer such questions, 265 church leaders, Catholic
and Protestant, completed a 100-item inventory, which was designed to measure both their degree of imagination and their stage
of faith development (using Fowler's six-stage model, which is
really only a five-stage model, since Fowler finds Stage 6 is unat-
tainable for the vast majority). By relating each subject's degree
of imaginative activity with their stage of faith development, I
was able to compare the relative strength of that relationship with
such other relationships impacting on faith development as that of
being a man or a woman, lay person or clergy, from a devout
home upbringing or not, mystical or not.

Two dimensions of imagination were measured:

Fantasy — our most pleasurable and playful imaginings in
which we escape into another world.

---

[19] Cox, H., *The Seduction of the Spirit* (New York: Simon & Schuster, 1973), p. 320-321.

Insight — our most reality-oriented imaginings in which we attempt to penetrate to the heart of matters, see things as a whole, and discover what meaning and value inhere in things.

Four aspects of religious faith were measured:

Stage 5 Awareness — a mature level of awareness involving (1) appreciation for theological paradox and mystery; (2) openness to the insights and values of other traditions; (3) mastery of one's own tradition.

Devotion — closeness to God.

Fidelity — readiness to serve God in the world.

Mysticism — meaningful personal experiences of God.

There were several statements on the inventory pertaining to each of these two imaginative domains and four faith domains. In measuring imaginative insight, five statements were used:

1. Metaphors are often truer to life than clear logic.

2. I like to search for the meaning of spontaneous imagery that arises unexpectedly from the depths of my psyche.

3. I seek to be aware of all of life's possibilities.

4. I use my imagination to discover truths that are inaccessible to my reason and/or my senses.

5. I read poetry to deepen my awareness of life.

Respondents scored each such statement from 1 to 4, indicating the relative degree of personal truth in each such statement.

In measuring "Stage 5 Awareness," seven personal statements were used. For example, "Appreciation for paradox is central to my religious thinking," and "I find it spiritually nourishing to discuss issues of faith with people who are committed to faith traditions very different from my own."

In measuring "Devotion," nine statements were used, for example, "I constantly seek God's will through prayer," and "In the last few years I have grown much closer to God." Subjects were also measured on the warmth and devoutness of their home upbringing.

All 265 subjects (there were four separate uses of the same basic inventory with different populations) were over the age of 35, half were over 50, two-thirds were male, one-third were clergy, and almost all considered themselves either middle-of-the-road or liberal.

Composite results from these four surveys are given in Table One (with Eigenvalues above 2.0 giving a measure of content validity to each category and Cronbach alphas above .6 giving a measure of internal validity or reliability to each category).

These results supported the following hypotheses:

1. Imaginative insight has a strong positive association with Stage 5 religious awareness.

2. This relationship of insight to Stage 5 awareness is more powerful than the relationship to Stage 5 awareness of mysticism or home upbringing or clergy status.

3. Imaginative insight also enjoys a strong association with religious devotion, just as powerful an association with devotion as that of mysticism or of fidelity and far more powerful than the relationship of home upbringing or clergy status to devotion.

4. Fantasy, in contrast to insight, enjoys a very minimal association with Stage 5 awareness and religious devotion.

5. Higher levels of imaginative insight are associated with a stronger positive relationship between religious devotion and Stage 5 awareness, a finding particularly noticeable among male subjects, where those with lower (bottom 1/4) levels of insight evidenced a negative relationship ($r = -.16$) between devotion and Stage 5 awareness, while those with higher (top 1/4) levels of insight evidenced a positive relationship ($r = .28$).

TABLE ONE
Pearson product correlations (r's) for key variables,
plus their eigenvalue (validity) and alpha (reliability).

Variables	Eigen-values	Cronbach alphas	Fantasy (r)	Insight (r)	Awareness (r)	Devotion (r)
Fantasy	5.09	.76998	1.0	.56	.31	.19
Insight	3.09	.76128	.56	1.0	.49	.37
Awareness	3.79	.79836	.31°	.49°	1.0	.16
Devotion	5.19	.82484	.19	.37°	.16	1.0
Fidelity	1.40	.62485	.07	.36°	.37°	.39°
Mysticism	2.33	.80980	.26°	.44°	.16	.39°
Female	single item		.09	-.02	.03	.29°
Clergy	single item		.15	.20	.38°	.10
Upbringing	single item		.04	.03	-.01	.26°

° = P < .001

These results present a very convincing "Yes" to the question I had posed to participants in the ecumenical conference on faith development. Is imagination important to faith formation? If by imagination is meant "insight," the answer is "Yes, really quite important!" Imagination's openness to God's free realm of possibility has received impressive support from science's realm of probability. God's Word made flesh enters our hearts through the filter of imagination. Human imagination, once freed from bondage to sin, becomes God's image-in-action.

Implications for Religious Education

When we are young, imagination is highly teachable, indeed, almost catchable.[20] It is also highly vulnerable. In a non-supportive environment, where fantasy play is deemed unacceptably frivolous by parents or custodial adults, imagination withers.[21]

What might happen in religious education if children ages three to eight were allowed, indeed encouraged, to play out the stories of their faith imaginatively? Such play could take the form of formal role play, with the teacher(s) assigning parts and being ready themselves to jump in and show how it's done if necessary. Or such play could involve placing play figures of Bible heroes in a free play area and encouraging children to create their own stories. Either way, imagination and faith would begin to interact. Either way, children would begin to realize that faith lives within a realm of possibility.

Religious education has always had the same aura of boredom about it that surrounds education in the public school, an aura that can be traced to the emphasis on didactic material in both arenas. Imagination can be silly but never boring. It is too innately playful. When children are confronted with a clown, or a cartoon, or almost any form of make-believe, their faces light up. Even so, in religious education, the light of God can become light-hearted when it is perceived imaginatively.

Western religions have been, as Carl Jung pointed out, basically extroverted; that is, seeking God's grace from without rather than from within.[22] Many educational benefits derive from such extroversion — comradery, sharing, reaching out, modeling, and imitating attitudes and lifestyles. Yet cultivating insight may ultimately require a more introverted format than any which presently exists in religious education. There already exists in Roman Catholic practice a valuable tradition of meditation. Such meditation can take many forms. People can listen to a Bible story, spend two minutes in silence trying to visualize what they would be feeling and experiencing if they were present within the story itself, then once again have the story read aloud to them. Or people can

---

[20] Singer, D. J. and Singer, J. L., *Partners-In Play* (New York: Harper & Row, 1977), p. 1-97.

[21] Freyberg, J. T., "Hold High the Cardboard Sword," *Psychology Today*. Feb., 1975, p. 63-64.

[22] Jung, C., "The Difference between Eastern and Western Thinking," in *The Portable Jung*, G. Campbell, Ed. (New York: Viking Press, 1971), p. 488.

simply pick up their Bibles and read a story, trying to visualize exactly how it must have been — scenery, characters, nuances of speech. Such solitary meditation may be the fruit of many years of practice with imaginative meditation in group settings, but its potential for spiritual growth is witnessed to by this account from a Catholic spiritual director:

> As we deeply remain with a particular Gospel narrative over a period of time . . . our experience overflows from our imagination and fills our deep inner selves. . . . Our affections are touched at a deeper level of vulnerability. A oneness grows . . . as our deep inner recesses and God's heart move together.[23]

Perhaps the unity of Fowler's Stage 6 faith awareness would not be as rare as it is if such meditations were practiced regularly.

But meditation on Scriptural stories is not enough. People need to enter imaginatively into their own lives, discover their own life histories as stories being writ either by themselves or in collaboration with God's Spirit.

A sixth-grade Sunday School teacher I know has always had at the beginning of class the sharing of "good news" and some "bad news" from their own past week's worth of living. The children become participants in each other's stories. Their own lives attained the value of being a story worth hearing. Quite often their "news" would take up the entire class period, with children offering prayers of thanks and intercession at the end for things that touched them out of each other's stories.

It is time for religious educators to find the storytellers within their communities and release them to tell God's stories. If children are actually to "hear" God's Word, a story well told becomes the perfect vehicle. Every faith tradition is full of wonderful stories, both ancient and modern. A good story well told nourishes the spirit of all ages — and gets remembered far longer than memory verses or theological equations can ever equal.

Theater needs to emerge, just as music has already emerged, as a form of religious education. It has been my good fortune as a church educator to produce six different versions of *Godspell*. All ages within the church family were able to respond equally to its imaginative treatment of the Gospel stories. People who would never think of the Bible as remotely interesting found themselves

---

[23] Conroy, M., "A Dwelling Place; Images and our Experience of God," *Journal of Ongoing Formation*, 6, 1, 1985, p. 13-14.

listening to the text from Matthew as if it were right out of Bill Cosby. Christmas pagents are the last surviving relic of the medieval enthusiasm for chancel drama. Much can be done with teenagers in religious education if they are allowed opportunity to express themselves dramatically.

The extroverted, didactic, and crafts approach to religious education needs now to be balanced by an imaginative approach that is at once both playful and deeply inward. Teachers need to be encouraged to engage their charges at this level. To be sure, not all teachers feel at home with such play. Many will prefer traditional methods. But just as children are taken aside for music with a special teacher, so they can have times when they are exposed to the joys and illuminations of imaginative play. At very least classrooms can be equipped with imaginative props and children allowed to enjoy a regularly scheduled time of free (entering God's realm of possibility) play.

Conclusion

Only through imagination grounded in God's Spirit can humankind hope to perceive, with increasing degrees of clarity, God's kingdom of pure and creative possibility. Once aware of this kingdom, humankind first must learn to wonder at its awesome freedom and mystery. Such wonder is the alpha of a redeemed imagination, even as heartfelt intuitive insight is its omega. By submitting to the reign of a realm of freedom, we ourselves become free. Ultimately, we, as God, will possess the necessary insight and freedom to live in terms of our highest possibility, both in time and in eternity. Religious education, to be true to this process, begins in wonder and ends in insight, enabling us to live in terms of our highest historical and eternal potentiality.

Dr. Loomis is youth minister of First Congregational Presbyterian Church in Prescott, Arizona, and a member of the adjunct faculty of Prescott College in the area of psychology and religion.

PERSPECTIVES ON CHANGE IN CATHOLIC RELIGIOUS EDUCATION SINCE THE SECOND VATICAN COUNCIL

Graham M. Rossiter

Mount Saint Mary
Strathfield, Australia NSW 2135

On his death-bed, in May 1963, Pope John XXIII spoke these words:

> Today more than ever we are called to serve mankind as such, and not merely Catholics; to defend above all and everywhere the rights of the human person, and not merely those of the Catholic Church. Today's world, the needs made plain in the last 50 years, and a deeper understanding of doctrine, have brought us to a new situation.

These words encapsulated the spirit of the Second Vatican Council. They heralded a period of unprecedented and irreversible change in the Catholic Church, the church which had been unchanging for such a long time, with its monolithic stability as proof of its truth.

While making their own personal adjustments to this "new situation" in the church, religion teachers in Catholic schools also had to change the approach to religious education. The old catechism method was seen to be too narrow. There was considerable experimentation to find ways of making religion "live" for the students and of meeting young people's needs. For many, the extent and the speed of the change have been confusing. Four prominent factors, among others, have been influential:

1. Change in the theology and practice of the church, so that on some issues it was no longer easy to pinpoint one, unequivocal, authoritative Catholic view.

2. Change in the focus or style of religious education, so that at one stage the emphasis was on knowledge of the catechism, then

on "heralding" Salvation History, then on "experience," "liberation," "personal development," "consciousness-raising," "shared
praxis," "faith-sharing," etc.

3. Change in the variety and scope of content ranging from
fundamental theology, scripture, liturgy, personal relationships,
psychology, sex education, social problems, peace and war, death
and dying, the media, and world religions.

4. Puzzlement on the part of religion teachers with the ambi-
valent response (or lack of response) of students; in other words,
the classroom problems were not fully understood, and there
were no simple remedies.[1]

There have evidently been many positive developments in religious education in Catholic schools. Even though in recent years
there are signs of improved satisfaction with religious education,
there is not yet a clear consensus about the most appropriate and
effective ways of teaching religion. For many school principals,
heads of religion departments, teachers, parents, clergy, and students there remains some disquiet about the quality and purpose
of religious education. A sensitive understanding of the problems
can be a first step toward an enhanced confidence and effectiveness in the teaching of religion; for this to happen, a perspective
on the changes in religious education is essential.

While the particular focus of this article is on religious education in Catholic schools, it reflects changes and issues that are pertinent to religious education in other settings and in different
denominations.

Perspective on the Changes in Religious Education

Now, with the passage of time, we are able to look with more
understanding at the earlier perplexing changes in religious education since the Vatican Council. The various approaches (keryg-
matic, life-situation, experiential, social problems, consciousness-
raising, liberational, community service, shared praxis) were all
concerned with finding a prominent place for the "personal" dimension. The catechism method, although it is still used in some
classrooms, was largely superseded. Within a few years, an ap-

---

[1] Changes in religious education were also influenced by other factors such as changes
in the church, in society, and in general education, the development of the media (especially television), the training of religion teachers, and the type of resource materials
available.

proach that had dominated since the sixteenth century would be replaced by a series of approaches that, in different ways, sought to engage students at a more personal level.

Clearly, the catechism emphasized the communication of religious knowledge — church teachings encapsulated in a question/answer format — though some would argue that it was more concerned with religious behavior and morality.[2] Nevertheless, personal faith was often strongly developed in people who were in Catholic schools in those times.[3] Just how much the catechism-learning influenced their faith, positively or negatively, is an open question.[4] Perhaps more influential was the context. Catholic schools were well integrated within tightly knit Catholic communities headed by priests.

The new approaches to religious education went beyond the aim of communicating religious knowledge and specifically sought to nurture and develop faith.[5] This is not to say that developing faith was not an aim of the catechism method. Rather, the new appproaches sought to evoke a more explicit, verbal expression of faith in religion lessons. In the early 1960s, there was an emphasis on an "evangelising proclamation of the Good News, seeking a faith response." Later there was an interest in changing attitudes through group processes. Other approaches emphasised a recall of pupils' life experience or attempted to build on "new religious experiences" in the classroom. "Faith-sharing," a verbal expression of personal beliefs and commitments, was stressed, and in some cases a special effort was made to heighten young people's sensitivity to issues in social justice or to engage them in shared reflection/committed social action. At other times, there was an emphasis on self-awareness and on psychological insights into personal development and sexuality.

---

[2] G. English, "First Catch Your Teacher: Reflections on Religious Education in Catholic Secondary Schools," *Catholic School Studies* 58 (1985) 2, pp. 45-48.

[3] See, for example, religion teachers' reflections on the changing church in M. Crawford and G. Rossiter, *Teaching Religion in Catholic Schools: Theory and Practice* (Winona, MN: St. Mary's Press, 1986), pp. 6 and 10.

[4] Although some would claim that the catechism provided a solid foundation for their faith, others say that the catechism did not help them think about religious issues and that the first experience of challenging issues in life (for example at university) resulted in their giving away the faith.

[5] A description of various approaches to religious education since the Second Vatican Council is given in G. Rossiter, *Religious Education in Australian Schools* (Canberra: Curriculum Development Centre, 1981), pp. 106-21, and in *Teaching Religion in Catholic Schools: Theory and Practice*, chs. 1-2.

Retreats and religious camps proved to be a great success story as far as the overall religious education in Catholic high schools was concerned. Although there was much trial and error still going on in classroom religion lessons, the enthusiastic responses from students on retreats was remarkable. In the informal setting of the live-in retreat, an intimate sense of Christian community often developed. There were very favorable conditions for reflecting on life, religion, faith, and the self, and for vital, personal discussions. An enhanced celebration of Reconciliation and Eucharist invariably capped the community experience. The voluntary retreats and camps attended by members of commitment groups, like Y.C.S. (Young Christian Students), were even more remarkable. Such camps had more scope for student involvement, initiative, and leadership.[6] At the same time, teachers found that, in general, attempts to recreate in the classroom the atmosphere and methods of retreats were unsuccessful.

The personal dimension of religious education was "at home" in the intimate communitarian setting of the retreat. Religion teachers often wondered: "Why is it so different in the classroom?" There were successes in classroom religion lessons, but the enthusiasm and satisfaction could not always be sustained through the whole formal religion curriculum. An appropriate and a generally satisfying place had not yet been found for the more personal side of young people's religious education in the classroom.

The different emphases in the new approaches highlighted important aspects of spiritual development in the life-cycle or in the church's ministry and tried to "inject" such aspects into classroom religion lessons. For example, there was the prominence of personal experience in coming to knowledge of God and faith — hence the "experiential" emphasis; proclaiming the Good News was a key aspect of evangelization — hence the emphasis on Salvation History; mature faith required a sensitivity to injustice — hence an emphasis on "consciousness-raising"; catechesis was a dialogue of believers — hence the emphasis on "faith-sharing" and "faith response"; mature faith and participation in the "Kingdom of God" required shared committed action based on a

---

[6] A more detailed discussion of the conduct of retreats and camps appears in G. Rossiter, *Beyond the Classroom: New Approaches to Personal Development and Religious Education*, (Melbourne: Dove Communications, 1978). See also *Religious Education in Australian Schools*, pp. 110-111.

shared reflection on the Christian story — hence the corresponding emphases in the shared-praxis method.

Identification of key aspects of spiritual development and church ministry was sound. However, the estimations of how these processes should be *effected* by the teacher in the classroom have not always been realistic or appropriate.

The new approaches were successful in part, but no one of them proved entirely satisfactory or for that matter comprehensive. Spiritual development and the way a young person journeys into faith are complex, mainly internal processes. They take place on a much larger stage of life than that of the classroom and are influenced by many factors such as the individual's own prayer, the home, adult role models, peers, culturally conditioned expectations of life, the style of parish life and worship that is available, and so on. The problem for classroom religious education was to find the *appropriate classroom contribution* to these personal processes.

The Distinctive Contribution of the Classroom to Young People's Religious Education

Through sharpening the focus on the role of religion in the Catholic school, we are now able to incorporate the best of the developments in the past while being much more clear and realistic about what can be achieved in the classroom. What is taught in religion lessons should ideally complement other aspects of young people's overall education in faith in the school and in the community. For example, in addition to the formal religion lessons, all of the following make distinctive contributions to young people's spiritual development: prayer and liturgy (the religious life of the school); voluntary commitment groups (the best structures for catechesis — the dialogue between believers); pastoral care structures; community service; and the sense of community in the school.

What has been lacking in the new approaches discussed earlier is an appropriate classroom "slant" or "contextual emphasis" within which the more personal parts of religious education and spiritual development can be sensitively touched and comfortably integrated. The most appropriate slant or context for classroom religious education is to base it within an intellectual study — one that does not suffer by comparison with the cognitive challenges and study structures experienced by students in other subject areas.

Although knowledge and understanding of religion should be emphasized as a basis for classroom religious education, it should also show how the education of the emotions, reflection on faith, development of critical skills for analysis, evaluation, and decision-making are integral parts of the process.[7] So it is suggested that an open, critical, inquiring study of religion will do more to develop faith, attitudes, emotions, values, commitment, and aesthetic sensitivity than an approach that tries to deal with these personal areas more exclusively or explicitly. Because development in these areas must come from "within" the person, teachers need to create an atmosphere of freedom for reflection and discussion so that students will not feel any subtle, but nonetheless manipulative, pressure of "requirements" that they respond and change at a personal level. In practice, one of the most stifling influences on students' personal involvement in religious education is a perceived "requirement" that they participate at a personal level. One way in which this occurs is where teachers consciously or unconsciously direct too much attention to students' emotions or personal responses rather than to a sensitive handling of emotive issues within the context of an informative study. An example of this problem is illustrated from a recent journal article:

> The practice of some well-meaning teachers has been to present nuclear and other issues in terms of the Arms race, the nuclear winter and the starving millions who have suffered because of the diversion of funds to military expenditure. I believe this is bad educational practice. Films like *The Day After* paralyse teenagers with fear or guilt. Similarly, constantly exposing students to videos of famine victims causes guilt or eventually indifference. It is imperative we put before them a theology of hope.
>
> [A more appropriate way of handling the issues makes use of] the services of some balanced, informed and articulate speakers on peace issues from Catholic Church agencies, other churches and social justice groups. When students are exposed to such speakers they have the opportunity to think issues through, to ask questions, sometimes to argue an alternative case, and to brainstorm about ways in which they can get involved to improve their environment.[8]

---

[7] A more detailed account of how a "slant" or "emphasis" on the cognitive creates the best context for effectively educating the personal domain (faith, attitudes, emotions, etc.) is given in M. Crawford and G. Rossiter, *Teaching Religion in Catholic Schools: Theory and Practice*, chs. 4, 5, and 6, and in G. Rossiter, "The Place of Faith in Classroom Religious Education," *Catholic School Studies* 59 (1986) 2, pp. 49-55.

[8] C. Brown, "Working for Justice and Peace in the School Environment," *Curriculum Exchange* 4 (1986), p. 3.

Initially, when religion teachers hear the recommendation that religious education should be an "academic, inquiring study with an emphasis on information-giving," some wonder: "Is this neglecting the affective dimension? Is this narrow intellectualism?" The answer is certainly "No." It is in the context of an informative study that the most effective attention can be given to the personal dimension. There may be a negative reaction to words like "academic," "study," and "intellectual." However, when teachers look into the issue more carefully, taking account of the complex place for faith (and other personal aspects) in classroom lessons and when they consider the wide range of creative methods that should be used, they usually come to feel comfortable with this approach. In fact, they often find that this view of religious education resolves for them problems that have hampered their teaching, their selection and development of student materials, and their planning of the religion curriculum. A sharper understanding of the place for faith in classroom religious education not only makes the teaching more purposeful, confident, and satisfying for the teacher, and more interesting and informative for the students, but also makes the work more valuable as an opportunity for developing the students' religious faith.

Just how faith is developed through classroom religious education and how teachers need to give special attention to respect for young people's freedom in personal matters are considered in detail elsewhere.[9] What will be considered here are some aspects of religious education that have been emphasized recently: shared praxis, decision-making for committed social action, and personal appropriation of the faith tradition.

Some Aspects of Shared Praxis:
Their Place in Classroom Religious Education

As Groome describes it, shared praxis is

> A group of Christians sharing in dialogue their critical reflection on present action in the light of the Christian Story and its Vision toward the end of lived Christian faith.
> . . . it takes place in a situation of group dialogue.[10]

Shared praxis is very suitable for a small adult commitment

---

[9] See the reference in note 7.

[10] T. H. Groome, *Christian Religious Education* (San Francisco: Harper and Row, 1980), p. 184.

group. As the "shared praxis group must constantly approach its task of discernment with prayer for the presence of the Holy Spirit"[11] and because it is strongly oriented to decision-making for committed action as a follow up,[12] the approach is an authentic catechesis for adults or youth commitment groups. Because the natural context for shared praxis is different from a classroom with about 30 adolescents who attend religion lessons as part of the school's required core curriculum, the approach needs adaptation for classroom use.[13]

A review of Groome's book in the British religious education journal, *New Sower*, in 1981, noted that many religion teachers in Catholic schools have been using aspects of shared praxis without explicitly using Groome's terminology. In some Catholic school religion curricula, the "Story of Christianity" has been given a special emphasis by making it serve as the structure for the whole high school religion curriculum.[14] One of the main purposes of classroom religious education is to familiarize students with the Christian story — how it has evolved from its Judaic origins in the Hebrew Bible, through Jesus, the early church, and on through history to the Second Vatican Council and to contemporary religious issues. Also, a variety of teaching methods offers students many opportunities for making connections between their own personal story and the Christian story. "Imaginative identification" and "imaginative rehearsal" are influential personal learning processes for young people at all times and can be availed of in particular teaching methods in religion lessons.[15] This can do much to make religion "come alive" for students while avoiding the problem of expecting *every* lesson to be highly imaginative. A consistent "personal" dimension can be given to religious education in this way without creating artificial expectations that students should be bubbling with religious enthusiasm every lesson.

---

[11] Ibid., p. 198.

[12] Ibid., p. 197 ff.

[13] A discussion of the different emphases in "catechesis" and "religious education" is pertinent here. For such a discussion, see M. Crawford and G. Rossiter, *ibid.* chapter 3; M. Warren, "Ministry, Catechesis and Religious Education: Implications for Youth Ministry and Catholic Schools," *Catholic School Studies* 59 (1986) 2, pp. 45-48; G. Rossiter, "The Place of Faith in Classroom Religious Education in Catholic Schools," pp. 49-55; and G. Rossiter, "The Need for a 'Creative Divorce' Between Catechesis and Religious Education in Catholic Schools," *Religious Education* 77 (1982), 1, pp. 21-40.

[14] For example, the religion curriculum in M. Crawford and G. Rossiter, op. cit.

[15] Ibid., p. 73.

One of the regular parts of a shared praxis unit is "Recalling the Christian Story and the Vision." It seems to presume that students have a prior knowledge of the origins and history of Christianity. There is a danger that if this method is followed exclusively, it might lead to a piecemeal, "jerky" treatment of the Christian story, recalling only those aspects of the story that are relevant to the issues being considered. Perhaps a systematic familiarity with the Chistian tradition is not only a basic need in a religion curriculum in Catholic schools but also a prerequisite for effective shared praxis.

Decision-making and Committed Action

If shared praxis were to be the only method used, religious education could become lopsided as regards decision-making for committed social action. Although on certain occasions a topic can naturally flow through to a class decision on group action in the school or elsewhere, this should not be expected to occur too often, or the students could feel they were being manipulated into artificial committed action. This could trivialize committed social action — it needs application in the wider life of young people beyond classroom and school. Also, balance is needed in limiting the scope for social action on the part of students. The advice of Fr. Starratt is pertinent:

> While students may provide genuine service to disadvantaged or handicapped people in the community, we believe that the focus should be on what the students learn from the experience, rather than on the school's efforts to change some unjust structures in the community.[16]

What precedes social action in the way of "empowering" young people and helping them become more informed decision-makers is a crucial concern of religious education.

> Young people can feel afraid of making decisions about their own lifestyle and commitments. They can feel that they do not have enough knowledge or experience to make useful decisions. They can feel powerless. Religion teachers can help them see that they *do* have power over decision-making in their own lives. They can learn how to acquire knowledge of issues which will enable them to make and stand by deci-

---

[16] R. J. Starratt, *Sowing Seeds of Faith and Justice*, Washington: Jesuit Secondary Education Association. Also quoted in *Catholic School Studies* 59 (1986) 2, pp. 4 and 9.

sions with a measure of self-confidence in their own autonomy. A critical, inquiring study of religion helps them learn that they need not be
overwhelmed by life's problems, and that these problems can be inves-
tigated and informed decisions can be made about them.[17]

Appropriation of the Faith Tradition

Shared praxis stresses the participants' "appropriation" of the
faith tradition. Making the faith "one's own" is an important part
of the development of faith. Appropriation of the faith is influenced by many non-classroom factors. Hence, religion teachers
need to be careful that they do not trivialize this process by pre-
suming that too much of it ought to occur in the classroom. Still,
there should be many opportunities in religious education for students to think through what their faith tradition could mean for
them personally.

Students are always making judgments about the implications
of their learning and reflections in religious education, whether or
not the teacher explicitly draws attention to this. However, if
there is always an overt emphasis in the teaching method on making judgments and decisions for action about *everything* they
consider, then there is a danger that this may artificially contract
judgment and decision-making from their broader place in the
life-cycle into a narrow "tokenism" in the classroom. This can be
perceived by the students as another new "hoop" the teacher
wants them to jump through rather than taking up the natural interest in evaluation and decisions on particular issues that they feel
strongly about.

Teachers can easily ask challenging personal questions about
evaluation and decisions within the context of an informative
study. For example, students can be asked to consider the personal implications and the challenges for the church arising from
their study of the Gospels.[18] However, teachers must leave the
students free to respond to such questions in their own way and in
their own time. Whether they respond there and then in the classroom will not be a good indicator of how effective that teaching
has been.

Where the processes of evaluation, appropriation, and
decision-making are formally and structurally incorporated as

---

[17] M. Crawford and G. Rossiter, *op. cit.* p. 13.
[18] Ibid., p. 76 ff.

regular parts of a teaching method in every religion lesson or unit of work, there is a danger that the teacher will presume that students will not evaluate, appropriate, or make decisions unless the teacher initiates the processes by asking the right questions. This can underestimate and patronize the natural capacity of young people to respond critically to the material they are studying, whether or not they inform the teacher of their views; it also devalues the material itself, as if it did not have enough power of its own to challenge the students. For example, the Gospels are not so abstruse that the only way students can see present implications is when prompted by teachers to consider them. The aim is to encourage the development of critical processes as a natural part of the life cycle. To do this, teachers often need to prompt, suggest, and point to possible implications. However, this needs to be done with sensitivity and selectivity, so that the students gradually become more autonomous in their own evaluations. What is done to foster this development in the classroom will then be natural and not artificial.

Comparisons with Other Curriculum Areas

This article has given some perspective to the changes in Catholic school religious education since the Second Vatican Council, by noting the changing emphases in the education of the "personal domain." Such an interest in educating the personal side of young people's development is not restricted to religious education; it has become a concern of many other curriculum areas. Hence a two-way flow of ideas should be possible. Religious educators should be able to learn from the ways in which education in other subject areas has attended to personal development, to decision-making, and to social action; aspects such as these are more and more being regarded as important parts of "authentic knowing." Also, teachers in other subject areas who are experimenting with ways of educating students personally in value-laden issues such as environment, peace, social problems, moral development, and personal development could learn much from the history of religious education. How to involve students personally without indoctrination or manipulation and how to respect their freedom are just as relevant in other curriculum areas as they are in religious education.

It is of interest to see how, in subjects like English, history, and social science, teachers' experimentation with more personally relevant learning is also moving toward positions of balance comparable with that noted earlier for religious education. For example, gone are the days when teachers in quest of creative writing would completely disregard the duller strictures of teaching grammar to encourage the more imaginative, exciting experience of self-expression. While they would not want to return to approaches that were purely mechanical, neither would they want to divorce the development of sound grammar from creative writing. In history, teachers are encouraging the imaginative participation of students in the events they are studying so that history would be more engaging than the "learning off" of dates and events. In the social sciences, the objectives now give much more attention to the development of the affective domain, to critical skills and decision-making.

There is no question that such personal objectives are needed. Few would advocate purely cognitive goals; yet there remains a gap between theory and practice as educators work out what are the most appropriate and effective ways of achieving personal learning in the classroom. An even more important question to resolve first is "What elements of personal learning are appropriate in the classroom?" What has been learned in religious education is quite pertinent to these developments. What will likely endure will be a balanced approach, which integrates the personal and the social action aspects within an intellectually challenging study. This mirrors the way in which the development of personal, social, and intellectual aspects are intimately related in the individual in real life.

Concluding Comment on the Context of Religious Education in Catholic Schools

Constructive future development of religious education in Catholic schools requires a perspective on past changes. This perspective helps educators understand what is happening at present and it helps them imagine the future.

Any action to improve the quality of classroom teaching in religious education along the lines considered in this article needs to go hand in hand with the development of suitable student materials and with the upgrading of the role of the religion curriculum in the school.

Although recent surveys of Catholic high school students in Australia suggest that young people are more satisfied with religious education in recent years than they were in the early 1970s, there is still a poor "image" for religion as a school subject that does not "count." It does not always have the systematic learning structures, the sequenced programs, the appropriate texts, homework, assessment, and official accreditation that students take for granted in other subjects. There is often a credibility gap between how important religion is said to be in the purposes of the school and how it figures in real practice in the school's curriculum.

If Catholic schools are to be serious about claims to have a special "Catholic" character, then they need to be serious about having religion professionally taught and assessed (as well as having a vigorous liturgical, spiritual, and pastoral life in the school).

This article has suggested that an understanding of the different emphases in educating the personal provides a useful perspective on the many, sometimes confusing, changes in Catholic religious education over the past 30 years. By implication, it suggests that there is no need to invent any new approach as a panacea or as a pertinent new trend. Rather, a perspective on historical changes in religious education should enable teachers to incorporate the best elements of past approaches into a balanced selection of methods. It would be imperialistic to think that any one approach should be used exclusively — and just as unrealistic as to suggest there is only one approach to the teaching of English!

Religious education at school is by nature a hybrid subject (Scripture, theology, history, personal development, etc.). It needs diversity in method to retain vitality and interest. Where the basis of the activity is directed toward thoroughly informing young people about their own religious traditions, other religions, and religious issues, the more personal areas of faith, emotions, and attitudes are most appropriately and sensitively educated. All of this needs to be situated in a school that cares for its students individually — a school where the values implicit in its everyday life are clearly Christian.

> It is not that the Gospel has changed: it is that we have begun to understand it better. Those who have lived as long as I have . . . were enabled to compare different cultures and traditions, and know that the moment has come to discern the signs of the times, to seize the opportunity and to look far ahead. (Pope John XXIII, 24 May 1963)

Brother Rossiter is a consultant in education of Christian Brothers at Mount Saint Mary in Strathfield, Australia.

THE EDUCATION OF THE APOSTLES: MARK'S VIEW OF HUMAN TRANSFORMATION

Walter Wink

Auburn Theological Seminary
New York, NY 10027

When I study the Bible, alone or with others, my ultimate aim is not information, but transformation. I see no reason to trouble myself or others with Scripture unless in doing so we intend to approach as closely as we dare to the numinous majesty of the living God. Why open this explosive and shattering book unless we are willing, not just to be added to, but subtracted from? Shall I read Scripture merely to be confirmed in my own good opinions of myself and my world, or do I let its first word to me be a negation of every prop, every presumption, every prejudice that armors me against acknowledging my pitiable hunger, even starvation, for the truth I need in order to be whole? In short, why come to such a book seeking simply the answers to the questions that I pose, without at the same time letting these texts call in question not only my questions but my very existence?

The dominant approach to Scripture, however, is quite different. Whether in seminaries or in Sunday schools, whether its method is historical criticism or hardshell fundamentalism, the common presupposition in biblical study is the banking theory of knowledge. What is desired is biblical literacy. The student is a receptacle, relatively empty, and the goal of education is to fill the student as full of facts as possible. A successful theological education, for example, involves the "mastery" of the "theological encyclopedia"; that is, the memorization and collation of what the faculty in each field considers the essential materials any literate M. Div. should know. This view of learning is cumulative. Unless the student has been very badly trained, the educational task is simply to add on to what the student knows, to keep pouring into the safe deposit vault of accumulated treasures of information ever more information, in the belief that the abler students at least will be able to draw down on their accounts when occasions arise. Very little premium is placed on teaching students *how* to think. Seldom is any question raised about the peril in which such an educational theory places the soul.

The soul is imperiled by such an approach, and I know of no better way to make that peril evident than by examining Mark's view of the education of the apostles. Any casual reader of Mark's gospel is aware that Mark is exceptionally rough on the disciples. Matthew and Luke repeatedly tone him down.[1] It will come as no surprise that Mark does not subscribe to the banking theory of knowledge. He does not believe the disciples are basically in good shape, needing just a strong dose of Jesus' teaching to get them ready for their tasks. On the contrary, Mark, apparently on the authority of Jesus himself, regards the disciples as blind men who are incapable of understanding either who Jesus is or what he is about. No amount of learning can correct this. They are blind, and they must be healed. Faith for Mark is not then the opposite of doubt. It is blindness healed. It is having one's sight restored.

Mark develops this theme all through his gospel. The very first paragraph features John the Baptist's cry for *metanoia*, a new mind. Jesus' first words echo John's: Get a new mind, for the Reign of God is at hand. Jesus' first parable, the Sower, portrays, among other things, the kinds of receptivity people bring to that Reign, and in the other parables that Reign itself fools and surprises the listener with its unexpected ways of coming. Jesus demands of his hearers that they become like little children if they wish to enter the Reign of God, and that means, in effect, to view all our accumulated wisdom in the vault as nothing — though it is not nothing, is in fact extremely valuable, but valuable only if we regard it as nothing. For only when we regard it as nothing can the new thing that is God's reigning overtake us.

Jesus' hearers, be it noted, were not biblically illiterate Americans. They were Jews who had already "banked" Scripture quite thoroughly. They knew much of it by heart. But if they were to see

---

[1] See for example how either Matthew or Luke or both soften Mark 4:38; 8:14-21, 29, 32-33; 9:6, 32, 34; 10:32, 35; 14:37-42, 50. But at several points Matthew and Luke enlarge on the obduracy of the apostles as well (Matt. 14:28-33; 15:23; 17:20; Luke 9:54; 18:39).

the new thing emerging in Jesus, they would have to count their store of knowledge as nothing, their sight as blindness, their freedom as a form of possession, and turn to God to be healed.

How easy it would have been for Mark to have resorted to an insider/outsider scheme, in which "the Jews" were blind but the disciples were sighted. But it is one measure of the greatness of this gospel that it is the apostles themselves who are pictured as the great dunderheads. Mark does, to be sure, have Jesus assert that the parables are only for those inside the Kingdom, while those outside will see and hear but not understand (4:10-12). But then Jesus has to explain the parable he has just told — to the insiders! They understand no better than the others. It is the disciples who do not comprehend the mystery of the loaves, the disciples to whom Jesus turns in exasperation and says, "Having eyes do you not see?" It is Peter who rebukes him for predicting suffering and death, and Peter again who, on seeing an actual theophany on the Mount of Transfiguration, blabbers about building booths. It is the other disciples who, while Jesus is on the Mount of Transfiguration, could not heal an epileptic boy, and it is the disciples who cannot comprehend each repeated reference to his end.

All this leaps out at us even on a casual reading. Mark has most artfully developed the theme of the blindness of the disciples, however, in chapters six through eight. Alan Richardson was the first to perceive the remarkable parallelisms in these chapters, and I am simply building on his analysis.[2] What we have, says Richardson, is a double cycle of symmetrical motifs:

1. Feeding of 5,000 — 6:30-44	Feeding of 4,000 — 8:1-9
2. Crossing and landing on west shore — 6:45-56	Crossing and landing on west shore — 8:10
3. Controversy with the Pharisees about defilement — 7:1-23	Controversy with the Pharisees about signs — 8:11-13
4. Syrophoenician woman (the children's bread) — 7:24-30	Mystery of the loaves (leaven of the Pharisees and Herod) — 8:14-21
5. Healing of the deaf mute — 7:31-37	Healing of the blind man — 8:22-26

This structural parallelism is present even in the details of some of the parts. Compare for example the two feeding stories:

---

[2] Alan Richardson, *The Miracle Stories of the Gospels* (London: SCM Press, [1941] 1959), 81-99.

Feeding the 5,000	Feeding the 4,000
a lonely place	in the desert
5 loaves, 2 fishes	7 loaves, a few fish
he had compassion	I have compassion
How many loaves have you	How many loaves have you
commanded them all to sit down by companies on the green grass	commanded the crowd to sit down on the ground
taking	taking
blessed (*eulogēsev*)	having given thanks (*eucharistēsas*)
broke	broke
gave them to the disciples to set before the people	gave them to his disciples to set before the people
and he divided the two fish among them all	and they had a few small fish; and having blessed them, he commanded that these also should be set before them
and they all ate and were satisfied	and they ate, and were satisfied
And they took up	and they took up
12 baskets (*kophinōn*) full of broken pieces and of the fish	the broken pieces left over, seven baskets (*spuridas*) full
5,000 men	4,000 people
dismissed the crowd	he sent them away
puts disciples in boat to cross to other side	gets into boat with his disciples to cross to other side

Such remarkable parallels could simply be dismissed as the understandable consequence of these being two accounts of one event, as is probably the case. But there are also several striking and, I believe, significant differences between the two accounts that reveal Mark's understanding of their meaning. The feeding of the 5,000 is set in Galilee and suggests a Jewish crowd. The feeding of the 4,000 is apparently in the Decapolis (7:31), which would seem to imply a Gentile crowd. The five loaves seem to be symbolic of Judaism, reminiscent perhaps of the five books of Moses, the five books of the Psalms, the five books of I Enoch and Ecclesiasticus. The seven loaves, on the other hand, invite us to think of the seven deacons for the hellenists in Acts, the 70 Gentile nations, Luke's account of the mission to the 70, and the Septuagint (named after the 70 translators of the Hebrew Bible into Greek). All this borders on the fanciful until we note several corroborating details: The feeding of the 4,000 explicitly states that "some of them have come a long way" and that they might faint "on the way" (*en tē hodō*, 8:3). It is difficult not to see here a cryptic allusion to Gentile Christians who were followers of "the Way," the first name of the early community (Acts 9:2; 19:9, 23; 22:4; 24:14, 22).

Several other details follow the same pattern. The first feeding specifies 12 baskets (the 12 tribes of Israel?), the second seven baskets (the symbol of the Gentile church?). And even the words used for baskets are different. The first is the *kophinos*, the Jewish kosher lunchbasket, which was so unique that a person could be identified as Jewish just by bearing it (Juvenal 3.14; 6.542). The second is the *spuris* (or *sphuris*), an ordinary fish or laundry basket in use all over the Mediterranean world. And in the first feeding, Jesus uses the normal Jewish table blessing, here translated by *eulogēsen*; in the second he gave thanks (*eucharistēsas*), the word used by Paul in 1 Cor. 11:24, with sacramental overtones of the hellenistic Christian eucharist.

II

All these differences, striking as they are, could still be passed off as coincidences were it not for the fact that Mark himself is at pains to draw special attention to them in 8:14-21. Here, after both feedings have taken place, the disciples have gotten into the boat without remembering to bring bread; "and they had only one loaf with them in the boat." Did they then have no bread or not? Jesus warns them of the leaven of the Pharisees and of Herod, to which they uncomprehendingly respond, "We have no bread."

> And being aware of it, Jesus said to them, "Why do you discuss the fact that you have no bread? Do you not yet perceive or understand? Are your hearts hardened? Having eyes do you not see, and having ears do you not hear? And do you not remember? When I broke the five loaves for the five thousand, how many baskets (*kophinous*) full of broken pieces did you take up?" They said to him, "Twelve." "And the seven for the four thousand, how many baskets (*spuridōn*) full of broken pieces did you take up?" And they said to him, "Seven." And he said to them, "Do you not yet understand?"

Understand what? By emphasizing the numbers and the different words for the baskets, Mark all but dares us to see in the two feedings a prefigurement of the Gentile mission, following the sequence in Jesus' retort to the Syrophoenician woman, a Gentile herself, just a few paragraphs before: "Let the children first be fed, for it is not right to take the children's bread and throw it to the dogs [Gentiles]." But in the feeding of the 5,000 the children of Israel *had* been fed first, and now there is nothing to prevent the

Gentiles from drawing near. Soon after this exchange with a Gentile woman, Jesus feeds the 4,000, exemplifying to Mark's audience the same pattern followed by Paul: to the Jew first, and then to the Gentile (Rom. 1:16; 2;9, 10; cf. also Acts 19:8-10). All that, however, is scarcely a mystery sufficient to account for Jesus' enigmatic question, "Do you not yet understand?"

A similar refrain concludes the narrative of Jesus' walking on the water. Having just fed the 5,000, Jesus dismissed the disciples in a boat. Then when he came walking on the water, they were terrified. Taking pity on them, "he got into the boat with them and the wind ceased. And they were utterly astounded, for they did not understand about the loaves, but their hearts were hardened" (6:51-52). What a strange ending! He has walked on water, stilled waves, and yet, according to Mark, they do not understand. And what they do not understand is not what has just transpired, but the previous story about the feeding. Why is the meaning of his walking on the water utterly dependent on the loaves that were shared out upon the hillside the afternoon before?

Why doesn't Mark just come out and tell us what he means? Why, for that matter, doesn't Jesus simply explain to the disciples what it is that they don't understand? What can be more frustrating than being made to understand that you don't even understand what it is that you don't understand?

Or is it perhaps the case that what they do not understand cannot be told them, because they would simply try to force it into the procrustean bed of their old presuppositions? Jesus is not just interested in pouring a fresh new content into their heads, but in emptying them, of displacing the old presuppositions, of giving them a new mind. He cannot achieve that, however, by exhortation to think differently, since their minds are programmed by the software of those presuppositions. All he can do is to induce a systems breakdown, using that strangely neglected educational tool, deliberately induced frustration. He can only leave them spinning in confusion until the centrifuge of frustration breaks down the old mental configuration and opens up their hearts. They are, in short, the sighted blind. Therefore Mark turns to the theme of blindness.

His first story of the healing of a blind man climaxes the double sequence structure of chapters 6-8. Looking back over that entire sequence, Jesus has fed 5,000, walked on water, confuted the Pharisees, healed the Syrophoenician woman's daughter and a deaf mute, and fed 4,000 people. On the heels of all that the Pharisees come to ask him for a sign from heaven. A sign! As if that weren't enough, his own disciples in the next scene (8:14-21) do not know whether they have bread or not, and are declared deaf and blind, a judgment which falls between the stories of the deaf mute (7:31-37) and the blind man of Bethsaida (8:22-26).

In the healing of the deaf mute Mark has taken the statement that the man had a speech impediment (7:32) and intensified it into complete dumbness (7:37). By so slight a shift he is able to evoke Isa. 35:5-6 — "then the eyes of the blind shall be opened, and the ears of the *deaf* unstopped; then shall the lame man leap like a hart, and the tongue of the *dumb* sing for joy" (see also Isa. 29:18; 32:3-4; Ezek. 24:27). If then Jesus does these things, is that not a sign that the messianic age has dawned upon them? Why then can they not see it? The healing of the disciples' eyes is as yet only half performed: They see people as trees walking (8:24). Jesus must now go back and begin the work of opening their eyes all over again. Hence the second parallel sequence starts in the next episode.[3]

The parallel narrative to the healing of the deaf mute in the double-sequence structure is the healing of the blind man of Bethsaida (8:22-26). He is healed and silenced by Jesus. That story is then followed by Peter's so-called "confession," after which he too is silenced by Jesus. As Richardson puts it, "The Blind Man of Bethsaida is none other than St. Peter, whose eyes were opened near Caesarea Pahilippi" (p. 86). And just as it takes Jesus two tries to heal the blind man, it takes more than one try for Peter to really see, for even though he does comprehend that the messianic power is at work in Jesus, he is still trying to cram him into the old categories. This is made abundantly evident when he rebukes Jesus for teaching that the Son of Man must suffer. Jesus' response is the most violent statement in the entire Bible: "Get behind me, Satan!" (8:27-33).

Two tries — the entire double sequence of narrative, manifesting his powers — and still the apostles cannot see. At the heart of all these narratives is the problem of bringing disciples to the sight that is faith. Mark must go to such lengths to delineate that problem because it continued to be the central problem of his church: How do you help people who have adjusted manageably to an alienated and alienating world to see that they are in bondage? How do you help the sighted see that they are blind?

---

[3] Ibid., 85.

III

In the light of all this we can perhaps perceive that Mark's so-called "Messianic Secret" was not, as Wilhelm Wrede suggested, merely a theological veil thrown over the gospel in order to hide the fact that Jesus was not confessed, nor did he confess himself to be, messiah during his earthly life. I personally do doubt that Jesus claimed to be messiah, for the very reason we are discussing here: No matter how hard he might have tried, people would inevitably have interpreted whatever he said or did in terms of the power-presuppositions of the Old Testament promises. But there is a deeper truth to the messianic secret that Wrede and others did not see: It was not just a strategy to avoid arrest, or a literary technique to explain peoples' failure to acknowledge him. For the secret of Jesus' identity is the kind of secret that stays secret even when paraded openly before peoples' eyes. The crisis of Jesus' ministry is a crisis of epistemology: Why do people not recognize a revelation when it is stuck right under their noses? This secret is not a contrivance by a redactor to save the appearances. It is part and parcel of the human blindness that makes the coming of a revealer necessary in the first place. As Paul so eloquently put it, "The god of this world has blinded the minds of the unbelievers, to keep them from seeing the light of the gospel of the glory of Christ, who is the likeness of God" (2 Cor. 4:4).

Mark's last explicit attempt to address this problem of blindness is the concluding event in the public ministry of Jesus, prior to his entry into Jerusalem. It is also the last healing story in the gospel: the healing of blind Bartimaeus. It comes at the end of a block of teachings on discipleship, in which three more times Jesus has predicted his suffering and death to the uncomprehending and incredulous disciples (9:12; 9:30-32; 10:32-34. See especially 9:32 — "But they did not understand the saying, and they were afraid to ask him").

Bartimaeus, who has never been a follower of Jesus, somehow believes that Jesus is the Son of David, an expression that has not appeared before in Mark. When he is told to be silent, as Peter was when he called Jesus the Messiah (8:30, 33), Bartimaeus only cries the louder. Jesus identifies the power that heals his blindness as faith. The story concludes with Jesus sending the man on his way, and the man chooses to follow Jesus *en tē hodō* "on the Way," thus confirming our earlier suspicion that the same expression in the feeding of the 4,000 was intentionally charged with meaning (8:3 — *en tē hodō*).

Mark juxtaposes this story with the preceding account of the sons of Zebedee wrangling for the positions of Secretary of State and Secretary of Defense when Jesus comes into his power. When they ask him to fulfill their request, Jesus asks exactly the same question of them that he will next ask Bartimaeus: "What do you want me to do for you?" (10:36, 51). The sons of Zebedee, his closest companions, disciples, and students, ask for temporal power in what they still persist in regarding as an earthly empire. The blind man, who has known only darkness and the dust of the road, asks for sight. Who here is blind? Who can see? What ought the sons of Zebedee to have asked for? And what distress, what shattering, what seismic upheaval would it take to make them change their request?

Mark knows the answer to that question, because it was a part of the historical record. It would take the death and resurrection of Jesus. That then is all he has left to tell. But before we leave this central block, we should revert once more to two of its key passages. The first is the story of Jesus walking on the water. For not only does that narrative end with a curious twist, it is packed with an unusually dense number of historical present tenses. Mark is fond of that construction, but here there is more than simply lapsing into the style of oral transmission. For it is the disciples who are living in the past tense; Jesus seems to be always in the present. Immediately after the first feeding story, late in the afternoon (6:47), he makes his disciples get into the boat and go before him to the other side, to Bethsaida, while he dismisses the crowd. And after he takes leave of them, he goes into the hills to pray.

> And when evening came, the boat was out on the sea, and he was alone on the land. And about the fourth watch of the night [between 3 and 6 in the morning — how long have they been out there rowing? — almost 12 hours!] he *comes* to them, walking [present participle] on the sea. He meant to pass by them [!], but when they saw him walking on the sea, they thought it *is* a ghost (*phantasma*), and cried out; for they all saw him and were terrified. But immediately he spoke to them and *says*, "Take heart, it *is* I (*ego eimi*); have no fear." And he got into the boat with them and the wind ceased. And they were utterly astounded, for they did not understand about the loaves, but their hearts were hardened.

Perhaps Mark is thinking, with a bit of allegorical license, of the early Christians in Rome. Jesus, he is saying to them, is no phantasm, he is the great I AM. Nevertheless he is only known through faith. Faith is no human achievement, nor is it simply subscribing to certain beliefs. It is the gift of God through Christ

to the helpless, who blindly grope in the dark night of their storm-
tossed world, toiling hard at the oars against mounting waves of
opposition, and who are ready to abandon hope.[4] To them Jesus
appears alive. It is they who are caught in the past tense, yearning
for his former presence. But he is among them in the present tense.
They would *know* that, if only they understood the mystery of the
loaves.

That brings us back, one last time, to the other crossing, when
they forgot to bring bread, though they had one loaf with them in
the boat. Yet they stoutly deny it: "We have no bread."

> And being aware of it, Jesus said to them, Why do you discuss the fact
> that you have no bread? Do you not yet perceive or understand? Are
> your hearts hardened? Having eyes do you not see, and having ears do
> you not hear? And do you not remember? When I broke the five loaves
> for the five thousand, how many baskets (*kophinous*) of broken pieces
> did you take up?" They said to him, "Twelve." "And the seven for the
> four thousand, how many baskets (*spuridōn*) full of broken pieces did
> you take up?" And they said to him, "Seven." And he said to them, "Do
> you not yet understand?"

Well, do you? Is there one loaf, or not? And if there is one loaf,
is it not enough to feed 5,000, or 4,000, or any other number? For if
the risen Christ is present in the world, then that presence can be
known whenever bread is blessed, and broken, and given to be
shared. The mystery of the loaves is nothing less than the Eucha-
ristic mystery of the risen Lord, living among us.

IV

Looking back over the whole two-cycled arrangement of Mark
6-8, we can see Mark struggling with the problem of bringing his
readers to faith. Using his sources carefully, and making his point
more by the way his narratives are placed than by changes within
them, Mark portrays for his readers the arduous struggle of coming to sight. But if people are not just uninformed but preformed
and even deformed — that is, if the problem is not just lack of
information but a *false* learning, a distorted, deceiving and even
perverted learning — then how does one go about educating them
— or, if I may be so unkind, ourselves? Human beings, according
to biblical anthropology, are not empty vessels needing to be

---

[4] Ibid., 93, paraphrasing Tertullian, *De Bapt.* 12.

filled. They are always already filled. They have already been shaped by the self-interests and collective experience of their own sector of the community. They have an interest-conditioned and experience-conditioned manner of seeing and hearing and reacting. Experimental subjects wearing stereopticons capable of flashing two different pictures simultaneously, one to each eye, report seeing only the picture familiar to their cultural conditioning. When a picture of a baseball player was flashed to one eye and a bullfighter to the other, Mexicans reported seeing the bullfighter and North Americans saw the baseball player. Subjects shown an anomalous red six of spades will experience vague physical discomfort but identify it as a six of spades. We tend to see what we are trained to see, not what is there. As Erich Neumann put it,

> A large part of education will always be devoted to the formation of a persona, which will make the individual "clean about the house" and socially presentable, and will teach him, not what is, but what may be regarded as, real; all human societies are at all times far more interested in instructing their members in the techniques of not looking, of overlooking and of looking the other way than in sharpening their observation, increasing their alertness and fostering their love of truth.
> . . . whether it is a question of not mentioning certain subjects or of not admitting certain facts, of behaving as if certain non-existent entities in fact existed or of saying things which one does not mean or not saying things which one does mean.[5]

To put it in biblical terms, the Principalities and Powers hold people in their thrall. "The god of this world has blinded the minds of the unbelievers" (2 Cor. 4:4). We do not simply lack information; we are the victims of campaigns of disinformation. We soak up a steady stream of propaganda and ideology whose intention is to *prevent* thought. How was it possible, for example, for most Southern Christians to justify slavery for over a hundred years, and segregation for another hundred? Why did their love and faith and compassion not guide them to see slavery and segregation as fundamentally opposed to the will of God? How could German Christians flagrantly champion or passively acquiesce in the genocidal policies of Adolf Hitler? Why are so many men having such difficulty today in understanding how

---

[5] Erich Neumann, *Depth Psychology and a New Ethic* (New York: C. G. Jung Foundation, Putnam's, 1969), 38.

women have felt oppressed by a patriarchal culture and economy and even language? And why, for so many millenia, have most women accepted their lot? Why for so long did the white Dutch Reformed churches of South Africa defend the separation of races as divinely ordained? Why have we American Christians supinely accepted the militarization of our society under the doctrine of the "National Security State," and how can we as stewards of the creation condone a foreign policy that is prepared to obliterate life on much of or possibly even all of the planet, in order to "preserve" our way of life?

Not that the problem does not translate as outsiders who are blind and insiders who have sight. Christians have not only proved to be as blind as unbelievers to some of the most terrible sins in history, they have actually given spiritual and political support to those heinous policies. We know, for example, that in only a matter of a few years we will look back in horror at the Reagan administration's policies toward Nicaragua or Star Wars research and testing, just as we belatedly woke up to the evils of our war in Vietnam. Why will we not wake up sooner? The central problem of ethics, it seems to me, is not why we do not do the good, but how it is possible for the Principalities and Powers to hold us in their thrall so fast that we do not even *perceive* the good.

We are as blind as the disciples. And the most damning indictment of all is that we claim to see. Jesus is clear about one thing: Those who know the mystery of the reign of God are precisely those who have abandoned all presumption to have mastered holy matters. They are like little children. They are those who continually confess their blindness, in order that they might be healed. They are those who open themselves to be untaught the delusions spun by the Powers That Be.

V

If we, scholars and students and leaders of churches and executives of denominations, are in fact the blind, how can we begin to be healed? Would we not have to begin all over again each time we come to Scripture, the way T. S. Eliot says we must?

> In order to arrive there,
> To arrive where you are, to get from where you are not,
>   You must go by a way wherein there is no ecstasy.
> In order to arrive at what you do not know
>   You must go by a way which is the way of ignorance.

> In order to possess what you do not possess
>> You must go by the way of dispossession.
> In order to arrive at what you are not
>> You must go through the way in which you are not.
> And what you do not know is the only thing you know.[6]

We would have to abandon the dominant paradigm of knowledge, the one which has so imperiled our souls. Under the tyranny of this image, the Western world has pursued knowledge out of a compulsion to control the whole of reality through emptying it of mystery. Knowledge in this view is like a truncated pyramid:

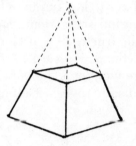

The goal is to reduce the unknown to the vanishing point, to finish out the pyramid by deciphering the whole of reality. This view has had no place for God, or awe, or wonder. God was merely the God of the gap at the top, and God shrunk with each new acquisition of knowledge. Mystery was merely what we haven't yet learned. Awe was rendered, if at all, to our own cleverness. This paradigm is not merely a mistake, it is a disease of soul. It is a lie.

What if we inverted that image, and saw the task of knowledge as exploration of a mystery that only grows in amplitude as we plumb it.

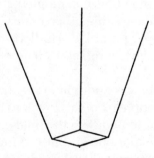

---

[6] T. S. Eliot, *Four Quartets* (New York: Harcourt Brace Jovanovich, 1971), 29. For a fuller discussion of the hermeneutical issues raised in the paragraphs that follow, see my *The Bible in Human Transformation* (Philadelphia: Fortress Press, 1973); and *Transforming Bible Study* (Nashville: Abingdon Press, 1980).

In this view, awe is the natural response to a universe that appears always ever greater. Knowledge is rendered humble by the recognition that the more we know, the more we know that we do not know.

But we do not begin our quest for knowledge with such an understanding. From our socialization as children through our indoctrination as adults, we are always already under the thralldom of the Powers. We have to be liberated, set free, exorcized, converted, healed from our blindness, in order to pass from the lower pyramid to the upper. And that means we have to die to the old way of knowing. We have to lose our lives to find them. Then, as we pass through this period of disorientation, in which we for the first time encounter the true reality of God, we enter a new dimension, where everything we learn reveals how much more there is to learn; where wonder is the only adequate response to the mystery that continually reveals itself as greater still.

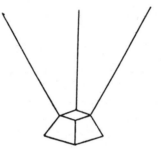

This new reality is incommensurate with the old. Notice the optical illusion: You can't even see both pyramids at the same time. From the point of view of the lower pyramid the upper is nonsensical — just a bunch of meaningless lines. No one locked under the Powers can see this other reality. Nor can it be explained. It can only be parabled, riddled, teasingly hinted at. Then one day, God just happens to a person. Blind eyes are opened.

That's really all Mark is about in his central section: trying to find a way to move people from this lower to this upper pyramid. But how God happens to people is the final mystery. It can never be understood, only experienced. But serving that mystery, and praying for it to happen, is for me the only worthwhile reason for biblical study.

Dr. Wink is professor of biblical interpretation at Auburn Theological Seminary.

ESSAY REVIEW

A NOTE FROM THE REVIEW EDITOR

Educating for Sexual Responsibility: Three Perspectives

Those who educate for sexual responsibility within the context of the local congregation more often than not turn to curriculum resources for guidance. Cynthia Harris, director of Princeton Seminary's Charles G. Reigner education library, and David H. Wall, assistant director of the School of Christian Education, Princeton Seminary, have compiled and commented on some 20-plus curriculum resources that are popularly used in the local congregation. This is an especially useful resource for the religious education practitioner.

Paul A. Westman, consultant for Lutheran educational materials, provides an update on current AIDS education resources. These resources become dated very quickly, and *Religious Education* is grateful for his offer to include his phone number for timely consultation with our readership.

Mary-Ruth Marshall, Erskin Theological Seminary's professor-elect of Christian Education, concludes this three-part focus on sexual responsibility by reviewing a highly popular investigation of the AIDS epidemic, *And the Band Played On*. The religious educational implications Marshall draws from this book are worth special consideration. — RHC

I. EDUCATING FOR SEXUAL RESPONSIBILITY: CURRICULUM RESOURCES

Christian Education: Shared Approaches published by Joint Educational
    Development
The following three resources are in the Youth Elect Series in the Living the Word approach.

The Search For Intimacy: A Youth Elect Series Course for Older Youth, 1981. This course contains six sessions for youth ages 15-18 and is designed to help these young people make responsible decisions and choices in the area of sexuality through an exploration of the issues in light of the biblical faith. Various kinds of methods are used in the sessions, and the material is dialogical, flexible, and inclusive. The outline of the course progresses from love of God, self, and neighbor, to decision-making and relationships of commitment and covenant. The course offers helpful advice in presenting the course to ministers, parents, and youth.

Growing Up to Love: The Meaning of Sexuality, 1978. The focus of this course for younger youth is personal value development. The six sessions are designed to provide information and resources in an atmosphere of open dialogue so that youth may explore the ethical, emotional, and spiritual issues related to human sexuality. The sessions are Sex is Natural and Special, Facing Facts About Sex and Our Bodies, Difference in Sexual Expression, How Does Society View Sex?, Personal Relationships and Sex, and Developing Your Own Sexual Identity.

Teenage Pregnancy: The Kids Next Door, 1983. This resource is designed for older youth and their parents to examine the roots of teenage pregnancy and our values as Christians. The hope is that education will help young people understand their own sexuality, and they will then make responsible choices regarding their sexual activity. There are six sessions, and the topics of contraception, peer pressure, and abortion are covered.

The following resources are in the Doing the Word approach.

Families and Violence: A Doing the Word Issue Guide, by Carol Wehrheim (United Church Press, 1985). This guide provides background and assistance in implementing any or all of the following three resources dealing with sexual violence. Models for doing education in this area are presented along with appropriate goals and activities for children, youth, adults, and intergenerational groups.

Sexual Violence: the Unmentionable Sin, by Marie M. Fortune, 1983. This book is for adults and covers the ethical and pastoral dimensions of the issue.

Nowhere to Turn, by Frances Johns (United Church Press, 1985). This is a book for children, grades 3-6, and contains stories and activities on the issue of sexual violence.

Sexual Abuse Prevention: A Study for Teenagers (United Church Press, 1984). This course is to be used as a supplement to a program on human sexuality. The purpose of this study is to provide youth, ages 12-18, with information and resources concerning sexual abuse and to give them the necessary skills so they can protect themselves. The course helps them to distinguish the difference between responsible sexual activity and sexual abuse. The five sessions cover the topics of sexual assault, confusing touch, incestuous assault, stereotypes and peer pressure, and media messages about women and men. Included in the course are sections on planning and resources.

David C. Cook: Christian Growth Elective

Created He Them Male & Female: A Biblical Perspective on Sexuality, 1979. This course offers a biblical sexual morality for high school juniors and seniors. The six-week elective series, which is to be preceded by a six-week study of Genesis 1-3, includes a teacher's guide and a student packet. The development of skills for moral reasoning and for personalizing a biblical view of sexuality are its objectives. The topics covered are God's good creation of the human body — male and female, marriage, sexual intercourse, overcoming the pressures of a permissive society, chastity, and love.

Kinheart Program on Sexuality and Homophobia

Homosexuality and The Church, by Mary Jo Osterman, 1984. A four-session study for adult groups who wish to examine the variety of perspectives on the issues of homosexuality and the church. The study is designed primarily for those persons who question the traditional Christian interpretations and believe that lesbian and gay persons should be fully accepted in the church and society. The session topics are Who Are We As Sexual Persons? Who is the Homosexual Person? What Do Bible and Society Say? What Do We Believe and What Must We Do?

Lutheran Church in America

Sexuality: God's Gift, 1985. An up-to-date course on human sexuality for adults from a Lutheran perspective. The six-session study gives participants an opportunity to define human sexuality, explore the biblical and theological foundations, focus on one's own beliefs and attitudes, and celebrate sexuality as God's gift. The course includes the topics of sexual orientation and sexism and comes with a leader's guide and participant's book.

Update on Love, Sex, and Life, 1974. This course is designed for junior high youth and comes with a leader's guide and student's booklet. It is divided into four units covering the themes of biological and psychological factors, sexual ethics, the biblical perspectives, and marriage. The number of sessions per unit will depend on the need of each group. Unfortunately, the photographs and some of the content material are dated.

The Lutheran Church — Missouri Synod

The Concordia Sex Education Series, 1982. A program designed to guide and help parents talk with their children about sex. The series provides information about the social-psychological and physiological aspects of human sexuality from the Christian point of view and is available in book form or on video-cassettes. The books are *Each One Specially* for ages 3-5, *I Wonder Why* for ages 6-8, *How You Got to Be You* ages 8-11, *The New You* ages 11-14, *Lord of Life, Lord of Me* ages 14 and over, and *Sexuality: God's Precious Gift to Parents and Children* for parents and teachers.

Presbyterian Church (U.S.A.)

Breaking The Silence: Overcoming The Fear: Homophobia Education, 1985. This revised booklet addresses the issue of homophobia, the fear and hatred of gay and lesbian persons within the society and church, specifically, The Presbyterian Church, U.S.A. In a series of articles and chapters, it addresses the issue, provides various biblical and theological perspectives on homosexuality, and offers models for homophobia education at various age levels within the church. The booklet includes a helpful section of questions for study and an extensive annotated bibliography on the church and homosexuality.

Roman Catholic — Ignatius Press

Love and Life: A Christian Sexual Morality Guide, 1986. A four-unit program for youth, parents, and teachers designed to teach young people the value of chastity and respect for the Church's teaching. Scripture, the documents of Vatican II, and contemporary material written by youth are used in the sessions. The course includes a student book, a parent's guide, teacher's guide, poster, and a video.

United Methodist Church

Sexuality: A Christian Perspective
This study series is for four age levels and includes the Guide to the Study Document on Human Sexuality, 1983, adopted in 1980 by the United Methodist Church. All levels refer to United Methodist beliefs and doctrines, and each level has a student book and a leader's guide.

Affirming Sexuality in Christian Adulthood, 1982. This course covers the sexuality issues that each stage of the life cycle brings while working towards an integration of these issues of sexuality as part of the continuing creating relationship between God and us.

Journeys: A Christian Approach to Sexuality, 1979. The aim of this course for senior high youth is to expand the knowledge about sexuality that the youth already has. But it does more than simply expand. Values are explored, and a perspective of sexuality in relation to maturing life is given. The youth will come away from this course affirmed in a holistic way.

Sex and Sexuality: A Christian Understanding, 1982. This resource for junior high youth and parents is unique in that it deals with the question, "Why sex education in the church?" and gives help to the planner in facilitating such a program. Its content covers the bases well: biology, problem issues, reproduction, and decision-making.

God Made Us: About Sex and Growing Up, 1980. This course is for older elementary boys and girls and is also recommended for their parents. It has good helps for the teacher in planning sexuality education in the church, and it gives the teacher an adequate degree of developmental understanding of children as well. There are seven sessions for children and six sessions for adults; it does not assume that adults know how to handle sexuality education with children but gives them the help they need to be responsible role models and nurturers.

Films and videos

Sex, Drugs & AIDS (O.D.N. Productions, NY, 1986). This is a secular video or film that is targeted for the youth audience. It comes with a discussion guide and a viewer pre- and post-test. The message is clear and simple: AIDS is hard to get. The video describes in a clear manner how AIDS is and is not transmitted and leaves the theological and moral implications to the viewers. It makes no pretenses about the sexual activity of today's youth but offers them guidance and information to make informed decisions regarding sexual activity. The blame for AIDS is placed on the virus and not on any persons or groups. (Available from ODN Productions, a nonprofit educational media company in New York.)

EcuFilm, an ecumenical film/video distribution service, offers a variety of materials for youth and adults in the area of human sexuality. Here is a partial listing:

Family Talks About Sex, 1978. For adults. Explores conversations parents have with their children about sex.

Human Growth II, 1977. For youth. Explores adolescent sexual development.

On Being Gay, 1986. For youth and adults. Brian McNaught talks about being gay in a straight world.

Sex and Decisions: Remember Tomorrow, 1985. For youth. Two young persons make a choice "to . . . or not."

There Is a Season, 1984. A 12-lesson study (three videos) in human sexuality for junior high youth and their parents.

They'll Know We Are Christians By Our Love, 1975. A two-part series for adults: "The Church and Human Sexuality" and "The Church and Homosexuality."

My Son, My Son, (Franciscan Communications, Los Angeles, CA, 1986). A film/ video with a guide targeted for junior high youth to adults that deals with the issues of homosexuality and AIDS and the themes of love, compassion, understanding, and caring. — *Cynthia Harris*. Director, The Charles G. Reigner Reading Room, Princeton Theological Seminary.

— *David H. Wall*, Assistant Director of the School of Christian Education, Princeton Theological Seminary.

II. EDUCATING FOR SEXUAL RESPONSIBILITY: AIDS EDUCATION RESOURCES

"Since there is no satisfactory drug treatment or vaccine for AIDS or the HIV virus at this time, the only effective means for fighting the disease is through education." — *Francisco Sy*, President, International Society for AIDS Education

Today's number one health problem and social concern has become a great challenge to many American congregations demanding both educational and pastoral action: how to respond to the AIDS crisis with integrity and compassion. Despite the external confusion over basic facts and internal controversy regarding religious and/or moral viewpoint, religious organizations are moving quickly to provide a number of print and visual resources for all ages. Articles, position papers, pamphlets, packets, and audio-visuals abound; new titles appear daily offering fresh data and experience. What follows is a sampling of resource as of press time in the fall of 1987. A word of caution is in order: Before sharing any source for study and/or action be sure to update its information with a reliable local or national AIDS hotline.

One source, which may be repoduced freely, comes from a church ministering to gay and lesbian communities. It provides an adult group with a six-week series on the topic *Do Not Fear, Only Believe: A Study/Dialogue Series for Spiritual Growth in Response to the AIDS Crisis*, 1986, Universal Fellowship of Metropolitan Community Churches. Addressed with references to the Gospels and letters of the New Testament are such subjects as fear of disease and death, homophobia, disease a punishment for sin, and grieving as healing. Also available is a follow-up program entitled *Resurrection Possibilities*.

A *Packet for Congregations*, prepared by the AIDS Task Force on the National Council of Churches, provides statements from mainline Protestant denominations, bibliography of print and audio-visual resources, glossary, practical tips on caregiving, personal stories, and guidelines for a biblical/theological approach to worship and action.

Talking to Your Family About Aids, a brochure prepared as a Family Resource by the Division for Parish Services, Lutheran Church in America, is by far one of the most helpful titles on teaching AIDS to children. Going beyond information, it seeks to give reason for presenting the subject and how to approach the AIDS crisis with preschoolers, children ages 6-9, and 10-12 years old. Explicit information is provided for pre-teens and teenagers. Added to this are helps regarding the church's message of faith and hope. The eight-page booklet concludes with a set of issues for discussion and an excellent listing of resources for all ages. Another Lutheran resource, *Ministry and the Threat of AIDS*, a packet for parish leaders, a cooperative project by five Lutheran denominations, is scheduled for publication. Contents will vary with each church's program; however, two unique titles for teenagers and their leaders are now projected: *You and AIDS*, a brochure for teens, and *AIDS and Christian Youth*, a manual for adult leaders of youth ministry programs. Both resources deal in an explicit manner with AIDS and other sexual matters of concern to today's teenager.

One highly recommended videotape is *Sex, Drugs and AIDS*, aimed at junior-senior high and college groups. Using a youth-to-youth approach, it is explicit in its treatment of AIDS, drugs, and safe contacts. A second video entitled, *The AIDS Crisis and the Church* produced by the United Methodists for television, features an interview with the surgeon general, a young Methodist person with AIDS, and a biblical scholar. A discussion guide is provided.

The publishers of Scriptographic Booklets have released a number of significant and informative titles for youth and adults: *About AIDS and Shooting Drugs*, *What Everyone Should Know about AIDS*, *What You Should Know about HIV and AIDS*, *What Gay and Bisexual Men Should Know about AIDS*, and *What Young People Should Know about AIDS*. This company has also released two new video productions, which deserve serious consideration as a basic resource for either a school or congregational program. — *Paul A. Westman*, Consultant, Educational Resources, Narberth, Pennsylvania.

For further information write Educational Resources, Box 882, Narberth, Pennsylvania, 19072; or, telephone Paul Westman, Educational Resources: 215-664-7040.

III. EDUCATING FOR SEXUAL RESPONSIBILITY

AND THE BAND PLAYED ON: POLITICS, PEOPLE, AND THE AIDS EPIDEMIC. By Randy Shilts. New York: St. Martin's Press, 1987. Cloth, 630 pp., $24.95.

Perhaps before the end of this decade, every local church and synagogue will have one or more members with AIDS or ARC. Each of you reading this review will know people with AIDS and will mourn the deaths of others. *And the Band Played On* is essential reading for all those who wish to understand the roots, beginnings, history, and likely directions of this human crisis.

This is a frightening book, inducing anger and despair in the reader; its analysis of human nature and the human condition is often bleakly Augustinian. But grace is also present in this story of human "courage as well as cowardice, compassion as well as bigotry, inspiration as well as veniality, and redemption as well as despair" (p. xxiii).

At least 1.5 million Americans are now infected with the AIDS virus. Deaths from AIDS, according to U.S. Surgeon General C. Everett Koop, are doubling every 13 months. This suggests, for example, that AIDS deaths in 1991 alone will exceed the totals of 1980 to 1990 combined. Koop expects 100 million deaths worldwide from AIDS by the turn of the century unless something is done now.

AIDS is the fastest spreading medical condition in the world today. There is no cure nor any known medical preventative or vaccine. Its mortality rate is 100 percent: An AIDS diagnosis is a death sentence. Most of its victims are young. Although the AIDS virus has been isolated, it is still not known what causes it or what causes it to become active in one infected as many as 15 years previously. AIDS itself is not a disease. The AIDS virus disables the immune system, leaving the body unprotected and prey to opportunistic infections it cannot subdue.

And the Band Played On narrates a popular history of the first phase of the AIDS epidemic, beginning in 1976 but with detailed focus on the years 1981-85. The book comes out of Shilts' investigative reporting on AIDS-related issues for the *San Francisco Chronicle*. It describes the way medical, scientific, national, international, and homosexual politics kept the band playing on in the face of human disaster. The author contends that the July 1985 announcement that actor Rock Hudson had AIDS, and his death a few months later, irrevocably changed everything and thus sharply divided the history of the AIDS epidemic, indeed, the history of America, into Before and After. This book tells the story of Before, although there is a brief epilogue that extends governmental, scientific, medical, and personal stories to 1987.

The purpose of the book is clear. The author says, in words reminiscent of the inscription on the Hiroshima monument, that the story "bears telling, so that it will never happen again, to any people, anywhere" (p. xxiii). This cautionary history indicts "an array of institutions, all of which failed to perform their appropriate tasks to safeguard the public health" (p. xxii): medicine, public health, federal and private scientific research establishments, the mass media, the gay community's leadership, the federal government. People died needlessly in this time of national and institutional failure, and the heroic figures are few, although valiant. That it could happen again is one clear warning of *And the Band Played On*; that AIDS is a continuing and global emergency is another.

Shilts narrates the epidemic's history chronologically, with several stories or sub-chronologies woven together in almost day-by-day accounts. This journal or newspaper-style structure makes the individual threads difficult to follow but also urges the reader on to the next installment of a particular sub-story. These sub-chronologies include the epidemiological story, punctuated regularly with the death knell — official figures of those stricken with AIDS and those whom it had killed; the scientific research story of detection and experiments with the AIDS virus, complicated by professional and international jealousies and empire protection; the clinical story of physicians bewildered by rare and unusual forms of cancer, pneumonia, and opportunistic infections, and the slow, morbid solution of this medical puzzle; and the socio-cultural story, characterized by embarrassment, indifference, ignorance, fear, prejudice, and rejection.

The stories in the foreground, however, are those of politics, involving all the preceding stories and others, and, even more memorably, those of individuals. The tragic linking of politics and people is seen over and over in decisions made or avoided by political groups, rather than on the basis of preservation of human life. Key AIDS issues were continually cast in purely political terms.

And the Band Played On is not a research document. It has no footnotes nor endnotes, as such. The author says that it is a work of journalism, without fictionalization, but adds that scenes, conversations, and observations were reconstructed for the purpose of narrative flow. One senses that reports of conversations and meetings often represent the recollections of one person or a few of those present. The author narrates or reports a history but does not attempt to analyze that history. The focus is almost entirely on the gay AIDS experience, with little mention of Haitians, intravenous drug users, hemophiliacs and others who received donated blood, or the sexual partners and children of these other AIDS victims. There is no indication of criticism of sources of determining validity. Indeed, the opposite more often seems true. The case is overstated, perhaps deliberately, at times. Historical research methodology is not the author's intent: he is reporting a history. This suggests that one should recognize the book for what it is — a limited popular history — and an excellent beginning point. There is no equivalent volume.

Developments in the story of the AIDS epidemic and efforts to stem it continue to be reported daily. This book will help readers to understand these developments and, of more concern, the degree to which fear, ignorance, prejudice, and rejection ensure that the band yet plays on.

Each of these factors plays a part in the development of an AIDS lexicon. Shilts, after Orwell, calls this AIDSpeak, a political language "forged by public health officials, anxious gay politicians, and the burgeoning ranks of 'AIDS activists'," characterized by euphemisms, globally inoffensive terminology, intransitive verbs, and syntax in word rather than deed. Its roots were not in truth but in "what was politically facile and psychologically reassuring" (p. 315). Words to be avoided, for example, included "victims," "promiscuous," "semen," "tell" or "instruct," "risk," and "infected." For these, AIDSpeak substituted "People With AIDS" or "PWAs," "sexually active," "bodily fluids," "informed choice," "making positive changes," and "exposed." "PWAs" is an example of the depersonalizing that seemed to flow on from the many AIDS-related acronyms, once agreement could be reached on what those acronymns should be. AIDSpeak denies the truth and offers falsely reassuring palliatives.

The book tells of some AIDS victims who found comfort, serenity, and a sense of hope in spirituality, often a return to childhood religious roots. Shilts gives a few examples of constructive speeches and actions by religious leaders but also devotes considerable space and criticism to conservative religious views and their vocalists. Their sermons or media statements on AIDS as God's punishment for the sin of homosexuality, and their calls for testing, quarantine, isolation, and/or exile of AIDS victims, are interpreted by Shilts as a perversion of religion, using religion to justify homophobia, fear, and hatred for a part of humanity. In "The City of God," Augustine describes the human tendency, in plague times, to blame and persecute its victims, casting them as scapegoats for what we fear and cannot comprehend or control.

Perhaps religious education has not found fault with victims nor urged their social exclusion, but it may be guilty, at least before 1985, of slipping silently by on the other side of the road. And the Band Played On emphasizes that knowledge, resources, and institutions failed in their response to the AIDS epidemic because of human ignorance and fear, prejudice and rejection. These pose important possibilities for ways religious education may minister to both the AIDS crisis and those who suffer it personally: AIDS victims, their families, and caregivers.

Throughout this book, straightforward, comprehensive, multi-level, and honest information-giving and education are seen as the solution to the ignorance of those at high levels of risk, and of the rest of society, all of whom are also at risk. Surely religious education, its curricula and settings, must be a part of that educational effort. More is needed than honest information, however. Religious education must speak out against false theologies and about the grace of God. Education's role in helping the church to be a community of reconciliation, servanthood, compassion, and touch may be its most important one: What must it be like to have human touch denied when it is most needed? Religious education may begin with language, speaking of AIDS and AIDS victims as God would speak of them: the children of God. Education may take the lead in a close examination of a society that leads to intravenous drug use, poverty, prostitution, lack of education, homelessness — some AIDS high risk areas — and work for the transformation and change of that society. — *Mary-Ruth Marshall*, Professor-elect of Christian Education, Erskin Theological Seminary, Due West, South Carolina.

BOOK REVIEWS

THE CREED. By Berard L. Marthaler. Mystic, Conn.: Twenty-Third Publications, 1987. Paper, 439 pp., $14.95.

The Creed is an unassumingly ambitious book, aiming at nothing less than a comprehensive exposition of the main contours of the Christian faith. Its purpose is explicitly ecumenical in that it attempts to uncover the convictions, attitudes, and values that are foundational for the Christian tradition. To do this, Marthaler rejects the once popular notion that "doctrine divides/service unites" and pursues the mandate of the Commission on Faith and Order of the World Council of Churches to work toward making the common confession of the apostolic faith one of the foundations for church unity. Marthaler argues that the longevity and wide use of the Ecumenical Creed of Constantinople of 381, often called the "Nicene" Creed, makes it a plausible focus for consensus on matters of faith. Most of the book is an interpretation of the Creed in the light of its biblical background and its role in the life of the church.

In order to defend the usefulness of the Creed, Marthaler argues that it does summarize and integrate essential biblical motifs. The Creed is rooted in the kerygma, particularly in the recitation of God's saving acts. Its tripartite structure corresponds to the biblical portrayal of God's three-fold activity in creating, redeeming, and sanctifying. Similarly, the organic interconnection of the articles of the Creed reflects the biblical testimony to the ultimate coherence of God's actions. When appropriate, Marthaler utilizes the results of contemporary biblical scholarship to support his contentions.

For Marthaler, the Creed is not only grounded in the kerygma but also in ecclesial praxis. He persuasively argues that the Creed must be interpreted and understood in the context of the church's life. Creedal language is not a neutral description of Divine realities; it is not a mere compendium of data about God in the way that a botanical treatise contains data about plants. Rather, the seemingly information-giving propositions in the Creed acquire meaning in the living of the Christian life. Creedal language is language which, like taking a vow or making a promise, involves the very existence of the speaker. In order to substantiate this claim, Marthaler analyzes the various self-involving functions which the Creed has performed in the history of Christian worship. For example, the confessional aspect of the Creed is evident in its original setting in the baptismal liturgy. Moreover, the Creed has served a doxological purpose, not only asserting propositions about God but also praising God. Finally, the Creed has served as an "identity-avowal," as a commitment to a particular way of life and to a unique community. These considerations demonstrate that it is the shape of the Christian life and the worshipful activities ingredient to it which gives substance and significance to the verbal formulae in the Creed.

If the book has a fault, it may be that Marthaler does not pay sufficient attention to the way in which the Creed's context has included the full variety of attitudes, passions, values, actions, and emotions, which constitute Christian existence. He tends to focus on the more formal, liturgical uses of the Creed. His analysis could have been profitably extended to encompass the ways in which the Creed has informed and been informed by private devotional practices, styles of action in the world, aesthetic experiences, and others.

Marthaler's understanding of the Creed and the way it functions would have provocative implications for the practice of Christian education. Extrapolating from Marthaler's conclusions, it would seem that many of the contemporary approaches to Christian education must be judged as being misguided, for many of them assume a faulty understanding of the nature of traditional Christian language. On the one hand, some approaches focus on the mastery of biblical and doctrinal "facts," presupposing a purely "referential" theory of religious language independent of the life of the community. On the other hand, other approaches that emphasize "faith development" or "telling one's story" assume that faith is an intrinsic dimension or structural dynamic of every individual's experience, which simply requires elicitation and cultivation. If Marthaler is right, both of these approaches must be rejected or at least qualified. For Marthaler, creedal language serves as a set of regulative principles to structure cognition, action, and experience. This view should lead to the reappropriation, with modifications, of the tradition of catechesis. Learning the faith would be like learning the grammar of a language, which would then furnish the medium in which life is lived. Learners must first be given help in discovering what the linguistic structures actually are, and then enabled to apply the principles to new and unfamiliar situations. The Creed, and Christian discourse in general, would provide the interpretive framework in which Christians at the most profound level perceive, experience, and act in the world. — *Lee C. Barrett III*, Professor of Theology, Presbyterian School of Christian Education.

ETHNICITY IN THE EDUCATION OF THE CHURCH. Edited by Charles R. Foster. Nashville: Scarritt Press, 1987. Paper, 106 pp., $7.95.

In the last few years, the Scarritt Graduate School in Nashville has taken a leading role in exploring the ramifications of multicultural experience for religious education. The present book is a record of a consultation held at Scarritt in the spring of 1985. Its three purposes were "to identify something of the content of the religious education experience of some of the ethnic constituencies of the church, to begin to explore their interaction in the educational life of the church, and to begin to clarify several issues that formulate an agenda for the church's religious education if it is to affirm its cultural diversity" (p. 2).

The plan of the conference, mirrored in the book, was simple. Papers were read by four representatives of different cultures in America. David Ng (whose paper was given by Arthur O. Van Eck), admitting the cultural complexity involved, discussed the resurgence of their backgrounds among people of Pacific Asian American descent and established one of the recurrent figures of the conference, that of "sojourners bearing gifts." Grant S. Shockley detailed the themes of oppression and liberation in the black consciousness and proposed an "intentional/engagement" model for Christian education in predominantly white churches with black constituencies. Charles R. Foster characterized the Anglo religious education experience as concerned with molding public values and attitudes, educating the conscience, and building a voluntary constituency. Virgilio Elizondo showed how a new culture has emerged for Mexican Americans out of Indian and European backgrounds and stressed its non-verbal and symbolic character, especially as shown in the devotion to the Virgin of Guadalupe.

Each paper was followed by a response from someone of another culture. It appears that the conference came to life when, in responding to Foster's presentation, Amos Jones, Jr. challenged its very purpose:

> Entering into dialogue is not enough to bring about a reflection of the church as the body of Christ. From my perspective, the history that stands behind the Anglo church and speaks so influentially to its contemporary setting leads me to say that the clay has spoiled in the hand of God. The only real possibility for the acceptance of ethnic multiplicity in the church's education is for the vessel to be broken and made over again into a totally new one (p. 73).

Apparently, the planners of the conference got more than they bargained for. From that point on the attempt was to deal with the polarities — the concept of mutual affirmation of the gifts different cultures bring and the concept of smashing the dominant culture (as has taken place to varying degrees in all the cultures represented), thus allowing a "new church, which provides our indigenous Christ for North America" (p. 92) to emerge.

In his summary, Foster called for developing a vocabulary affirming cultural diversity as a gift of God, discovering new images for the church's education to guide its efforts, and incorporating ways of religious learning (ritual, story, music, the dynamics of the common life, and ordered learning) that are indigenous to various ethnic and cultural communities (pp. 96-106).

The explosive factor here is a fact of American life — a dominant (if very mixed and immobilized) culture in a situation of pluralism, where the movement toward cultural affirmation and identity is replacing acceptance of cultural positioning as slaves and underdogs. Three possibilities emerge. First, the dominant culture enters into limited dialogue with other cultures and incorporates their values and ways into its views and ways of doing religious education. Second, recognizing that the "dominant culture" no longer occupies that position, a dialogue of "mutual affirmation and gift-bearing" is initiated in the search for a new multicultural approach to religious education. Third, the dominant culture is broken, and a new culture, with its new religious education approaches, is allowed to arise. The book takes us to the brink of decision among the three.

But it does not get as deeply into the process as was intended. The problem is the lack of cultural identity manifested among the various papers. Assimilation has gone so far in the case of Pacific Asian Americans that a cultural identity is something that almost has to be reinvented. In the case of the black experience, there is no trace of original cultural roots. In their place, the present culture is almost totally a response to the experience of North American oppression. As one reads the account of Anglo religious education experience, much that is recounted is already past and gone. The Mexican American experience is already a cultural amalgam. But there is cultural richness in each of these realms of experience, resources that the book only sketches briefly and does not explore in depth.

A hint of direction may be the observation a counselor friend of mine once made while dealing with a couple's marriage problems: "If they would only stop looking at each other, and both turn and look in the same direction!" Different cultures bring their various insights to the study of the Bible. Different cultures bring their various methods and perspectives to bear on the specific problems that plague us as a people. It's worth trying. — D. *Campbell Wyckoff*, Professor of Christian Education, Emeritus, Princeton Theological Seminary.

THE PARENT'S HANDBOOK: Systematic Training for Effective Parenting. By Don Dinkmeyer, Ph.D. and Gary D. McKay, Ph.D. Circle Pines, Minnesota: American Guidance Service, 1982. Paper, 121 pp., $9.95.

The *Parent's Handbook* serves as the focal point of the Systematic Training for Effective Parenting (STEP) program. The program has as its goals aiding parents in reducing parent/child conflict and raising responsible, self-reliant, self-disciplined children. Toward the accomplishment of these goals, the *Handbook* contributes a great deal, being used both in the home by parents and as the "textbook" for the parents' support groups for which the program is geared.

In nine concise chapters, the book moves from such topics as understanding your child's behavior/misbehavior, building your child's sense of self-worth, communication — both talking and listening to your child — to applying a method of discipline designed to develop responsibility. This method of discipline is referred to as "natural and logical consequences," a term attributed to Rudolf Dreikurs. Each chapter follows a set format: explanation of the topic principles, review questions for that topic, a problem situation for use in the parents' group, and an activity for the coming week that brings into focus the principles discussed in that chapter. In addition, each chapter has chart(s) summarizing the topic principles, a "points to remember" chart for easy reference, and a one-page assessment sheet for charting one's progress in each of the topic areas.

As a church educator, I found the emphasis on dealing with children from a basis of mutual respect most encouraging. The parent/child relationship is seen as one of equality, not in terms of knowledge or ability but in terms of human worth and dignity. Effective parenting should stress the well being of both the child and the parent and the building of positive relationships. These emphases are found in the *Handbook*. The fact that this is a very practical, clearly written work is also in its favor. Parents need both sound theory and sound practice. In its movement from discussion of principles through problem situations and activities to a concise, specific assessment sheet to chart one's parenting progress, this work provides for those needs. The topics covered speak to the areas of concern expressed by today's parents and give usable, practical advice on how to make parenting the joyous relationship it should be.

There are many parenting programs available these days, and to sway opinion for one over another is not my aim here. But as religious educators we do owe some responsibility to the nurturing of family well being. Some of us may be asked to recommend programs and/or lead parents' groups and, therefore, need to be aware of what is "out there." The STEP program emphasizes many ideas basic to Judeo-Christian traditions, specifically that we are beings of equality in worth and dignity and that we all need and want to be treated with respect. If we are treated with respect, we are more likely to treat others in a like manner. As Christians are we not taught to do unto others as we would have them do unto us and thereby give witness to God's love and care through the example of our own lives and relationships? If as parents we strive to be responsible in our parenting and work to instill respect and a sense of self-worth in our children, will they not be more likely to see themselves as worthy and to treat others in a respectful fashion? If as the church we wish to encourage and form responsible Christians, then we need to aid parents in the upbringing of responsible children.

The STEP program is not the only parenting program in town and the *Parent's Handbook* is not the last word in parenting strategy, but both together are certainly worth a careful look. — *Julia Lehmann*, Director of Christian Education, First Presbyterian Church, Rockingham, North Carolina.

THE PSYCHOLOGY OF RE-EDUCATION. By Paul Diel. Translated by Raymond Rosenthal. Boston: Shambhala Publications, Inc., 1987. Cloth, 253 pp., $27.50.

Paul Diel (1893-1972) was a pioneering French psychologist within the psychodynamic tradition of Freud, Adler, and Jung. Over the past ten years his numerous books have been steadily translated into English, the latest of which is *The Psychology of Re-education* (originally published in 1962). Presupposing a substantial background on the language and concepts of psychodynamic psychology, this book is a highly technical and dense application of his earlier work on human motivation to the tasks of "education" and "re-education." Diel's scope is the dynamics and conditions of healthy child development ("education"), the dynamics by which such development is falsified, and the principles for psychotherapeutic intervention in the cases of deeply disturbed development in children and adolescents (psychotherapy as "re-education" into the unfolding of healthy development).

Though clearly within the psychodynamic tradition, Diel's approach to human behavior is unique. He begins this work with a description of the inner functioning of the psychic system, the apprehension of which may necessitate some familiarity with his earlier works, especially *The Psychology of Motivation* (1948). Diel's fundamental interest is in human motivation, namely, those drives and needs whose search for satisfaction motivate and determine all human behavior. Objects which bring satisfaction to these drives are validated by the mind and become values that guide subsequent behavior. Critically synthesizing Freud, Adler, and Jung, Diel sees the primary drives of human behavior as threefold: sexual (Freud), material (Adler), and spiritual (Jung).

Ideal human development occurs when behavior is motivated by values that satisfy the spiritual drive of the psyche and sublimate the sexual and material drives. Though its specific content is not detailed, Diel describes this spritual drive as a compelling need that one's thought, actions, and feelings be adapted in "harmony" with authentic values of truth, goodness, and beauty. Behavior in accordance with these values generates spontaneous joy, while behavior that violates them generates anguish. The development of the spiritual drive would occur naturally in an environment that firmly embodies these authentic values and patiently guides the child in choosing for them. This "education" is a shaping of character by which the child learns to make true and good decisions on the basis of its satisfaction of an implicit spiritual drive.

When this spiritual drive is left unsatisfied or undeveloped, it becomes repressed, and the psyche is motivated by a synthesis of a perverted sexual drive and a destructive drive for social dominance. Development is thus falsified, and the psyche makes choices upon values that are incapable of eliciting spiritual satisfaction. In the midst of a materialistic, hedonistic, and morally ambiguous culture, such falsification is inevitable.

Liberation from such false motivation occurs through a form of self-transcendence where, through the power of a lucid mind, one is able to see the ultimately dissatisfying nature of one's behavior, master the self-defeating sexual and material drives, and make value-filled decisions on the basis of the immanent spiritual drive. Because the spiritual intuition exists within the psyche, liberating self-determination can occur through penetrating introspection. In the event of serious developmental falsification, however, re-education through psychotherapy is necessary.

Diel's book is an advanced work on dynamic psychology. As such, it was not written for the lay person nor does it explicitly treat the issues of religious education. The educator with an extensive background and interests in the psychological motivations of human behavior may find this book evocative, though dense and complex. Its adaptation to the specific concerns of religious education would necessitate theological assessment. While Diel's emphasis on value-filled character formation is exemplary, his faith in the spiritual instinct of the psyche, the mind's capacity to choose for spiritual values over self-deceptive ones, and the redemptive power of introspection seem optimistic. Without theological reassessment, Diel's approach would reduce the spiritual to the level of the intrapsychic, thus rendering self-determination an impossibility. — *Frank Rogers, Jr.*, Doctoral Candidate, Princeton Theological Seminary.

RELIGIOUS EXPERIENCING: WILLIAM JAMES AND EUGENE GENDLIN. By John J. Shea. Lanham, MD: University Press, 1987. Paper. 145 pages, $10.75.

THE GRACIOUS MYSTERY: FINDING GOD IN ORDINARY EXPERIENCE. By James J. Bacik. Cincinnati: St. Anthony Messenger Press, 1987. Paper, 141 pages, $5.95.

Since Schleiermacher, "feeling" has gained prominence as the core of religion, from which concepts arise; and with the rise of phenomenological method, "experience" has become a locus of the religious. The question within this point of view is, What *are* religious feelings and *how* are they central? Or, what *is* religious experience? Both Shea and Bacik enter the phenomenological discussion of these questions, from different perspectives, with different arguments, and writing to different audiences.

Shea's book approaches the role of feeling in religious experience by combining the phenomenological religious thought of William James with the psychological theory of Eugene Gendlin. Specifically, he accepts James' nascent idea of feeling as the primary, deep source of religion, then elaborates this through Gendlin's concrete process of locating and transforming the experiential core within the person. Religious experiencing emerges as a process of inner growth that can be intentionally directed. As Shea reads James, "feeling" is closely tied to the openness that renders one receptive to unexpected life-changing experiences. Religious feeling is a particular form of this mystical experience — a process of being open to experience the divine. Religious response is the person's feeling in relation to the experienced divine. What the divine is, or what feelings are clearly "religious," neither James nor Shea can say.

At this point Shea turns to Gendlin's contemporary psychological therapy, as continuation and concrete elaboration of James' idea. For Gendlin, as for James, experience is not an object but a sense or feeling; when people undergo personal change, this feeling process is intensified and heightened. Gendlin suggests that change can be encouraged through the therapeutic process of "focusing," which brings present experience into clear awareness and allows the person to be carried further by experience.

Shea's conclusion from juxtaposing James and Gendlin is that "religious experience" is a phenomenon that can be developed through intentional processes. He is then concerned with the implications of such a process for ministries, including religious education. Here he proposes a paradigmatic shift from concern for instructional content to focus on each person's religious experiencing and its meaning. The goal is not knowledge but religious experiencing.

Shea's work suggests a harmony of religious and psychological phenomenology. The juxtaposition of James and Gendlin, obviously designed to bring "religious" into the therapeutic experiencing model, is at times forced, so the reader questions the depth of fit between the two theories. Might some basic disagreeing assumptions underlie religious phenomenology and psychological therapy?

These doubts aside, the book does attempt an argument about feeling and experiencing in religion, different from, yet reminiscent of, John Wilson's *Education in Religion and the Emotions*. The argument can serve to advance discussion of affective religious education, and Shea's proposed model is a laudable endeavor.

Bacik's book is a more popular treatment, outlining a contemporary American spirituality, responsive to the paradoxes of life, based in Karl Rahner's theology. The book is a collection of essays in two sections: Part I offers a theoretical framework for cultivating personal awareness of self and God, and Part II exemplifies the model through stories of deepened religious experiencing.

Like Shea, Bacik believes we can systematically attune the person to the religious. However, the processes he suggests, and their sources, differ from Shea's pure phenomenological psychology. Unlike Shea, Bacik locates the heart of the religious *in* second-level reflection, rather than in the immediacy of experience. For Bacik, it is the ability to distance, conceptualize, and symbolize our experience in the imagination that is the source of our religion, not pure immediacy and feeling. For Bacik, the divine can be clearly identified as the Mystery of our lives (Shea wishes to avoid a particular conceptualization of the divine), so the cultivation of religious feeling lies in developing experiential response to this Mystery. The process thus emerges as more eclectic than Shea's therapeutic "focusing," to include self-acceptance, responses to contemporary theological issues, living fully in the present moment, being realistic about the world yet finding signs of God's presence, and intentionally focusing on the deep mysteries in ordinary experiences.

Bacik's book is not a conceptual argument but a series of phenomenological reflections, similar to much of Henri Nouwen's work. It is probably of more interest to lay churchpersons than Shea's treatise, with a Roman Catholic appeal. It suffers from some linguistic, conceptual confusion (especially among spirit, imago Dei, and religion), but the overall vision is readily grasped. — *Pamela*

Mitchell, Professor of Christian Education, United Theological Seminary, Dayton, Ohio.

EDUCATION IN RELIGIOUS UNDERSTANDING. By John B. Wilson and Samuel M. Natale. New York: University Press of America, 1987. Paper 75 pp., $9.50.

In this brief work authors John Wilson, a fellow at Mansfield College, Oxford, and frequent contributor in the areas of religious and moral education, and Sam Natale, now professor of business and society at the Hagan School of Business in Iona College, New York, undertake a new approach to the general topic of religious education. Funded by the Foundation for Education in Religion and Morality, a nonprofit corporation whose board members represent both the U.S. and the United Kingdom, this first report under directors Wilson and Natale does not examine programs, curriculum, content, or methods but explores the very meaning of "education in religion." The foundation's and the report's work rests upon two premises, "prima facie facts" in the authors' words: 1) religious and other similar outlooks are important to individuals and societies; 2) no society has developed a satisfactory way to educate young people into religion.

The report is divided into two parts. Part II is a summary of a survey of 500 teachers, parents, and pupils related to secondary schools in the U.S. and 500 in the U.K. Though by no means exhaustive, the research indicated that the majority thought education in religion was not only a desirable objective but should receive government support. Part I provides the rationale for what the authors mean by education in religion. Finally, the report includes a separate essay by Natale on moral education in a corporate setting, which seems more like an excursion than an integral part of the report.

For the authors, to educate means to convince of the reasonableness of one's position. Acknowledging that such a position raises troubling questions, Wilson and Natale advance their main thesis that religion rests primarily upon those emotions associated with religious experience and upon the activity of worship. Religious education, then, is part of the education of the emotions but needs the criteria of rationality, as with education *in* any area of study such as literature, history, and so on.

On the one hand Wilson and Natale want to avoid religious education that indoctrinates or "(more feebly)" keeps "the pot lukewarm by giving our children some vaguely-conceived instruction in matters contingently connected with certain religions, but not central to religion as a whole" (p. 33). Rather, for them the aim of religious education is to produce "autonomous and rational adults, who can make reasonable choices in the sphere of religion and the emotions" (p. 52). In this scheme the specific *content* or *method* of religious education is open-ended, depending on how much it contributes to the aim just mentioned. The authors concede that this aim "may" be achieved best by making a good deal of use of Christianity in quasi-Christian countries. But that may not be the case. Regardless, their suggestion would be to organize contents and methods around concepts that form the "stuff" of religion — worship, awe, guilt, forgiveness, and others.

From their initial survey sample and after the development of an argument for "education *in* religion" rather than *about* religion, the authors propose further research and public education in a non-partisan approach to religious education. Their efforts, both the argument for government support and their analysis of education *in* religion, should provide gist for encounters among religious educators of every religious tradition.

However, the basic argument raises a number of puzzling questions. I never found a clear indication of what the "reasonableness" of religion involved. What is the relationship between education in those emotions, which are the "stuff" of religion, and the aim of producing "autonomous and rational adults who can make reasonable choices in the sphere of religion and emotions?" Although an interesting possible relation seems to exist, the argument needs much further development. Wilson and Natale rest their discussion heavily on a psychoanalytic model, evident in several examples and perhaps most strikingly in this remark: "The relevant type of [religious] education is in general more analogous to certain types of psychotherapy than to subject-teaching." Granted that their "type" is analogous, but is religious education itself? Or, for that matter, why is religion primarily a matter of the emotions? What about the role of symbols and imagination? What "type" of religious education would an anthropological framework provide?

In spite of their sexist language, which seems strikingly out of date in the late 1980s, Wilson and Natale provide a cogent position that deserves more discussion and debate. In their attempt to develop a concept of education *in* religion, which is non-partisan and thus capable of government support in a pluralistic society, they have raised important questions for religious educators who argue for the centrality of any tradition's perspective. Are our religious perspectives secondary impositions on basic emotions, or is there a more dynamic relationship between emotions and beliefs which needs amplification here? — *Gary L. Chamberlain*, Associate Professor, Seattle University.

GOD'S CHOICE. By Alan Peshkin. Chicago: University of Chicago Press, 1986. Cloth, 350 pp., $24.95.

Alan Peshkin, a professor of education at the University of Illinois in Urbana-Champaign, has completed the third in a series of field research studies that examine the nature of schooling in various settings.

Peshkin, a Jew, speaks openly of his first attempts to find a Christian school in which to observe. (He clearly distinguishes between a Christian school and a parochial school, with "Christian" being the narrower term.) He tried in 1978 and again in 1979 to find a school in Urbana-Champaign, only to fail because he was not a Christian. He was able to do pilot studies in Roman Catholic, Lutheran, and Seventh-Day Adventist schools, but was refused opportunity for extended study in any of three fundamentalist schools. A refusing pastor said: "You're like a Russian who says he wants to attend meetings at the Pentagon —just to learn. . . . No matter how good a person you are, you will misrepresent my school because you don't have the Holy Spirit in you. First, become a child of the King, and then you can pursue your study of Christian schools."

The purpose of Peshkin's study was to examine the relationship between religious doctrine and educational practice. He finally found his school in the central Illinois community of Hartney (a pseudonym) at Bethany Baptist

Academy (another pseudonym). He spent 18 months involved with the church and school from Sunday morning through Friday afternoon. The book is a report of what he found.

Bethany Baptist Academy had an enrollment of 350 in kindergarten through 12th grade at the time when Peshkin studied it. Bethany leaders, like those in most fundamentalist schools, believe that church and school are one. Consequently, the pastor was deeply involved in the direction of the school, though the day-to-day operation was left to a headmaster.

One chapter, entitled "The Dictates of Doctrine," outlines the doctrinal tenets that direct the program at Bethany. Peshkin states

> If most public school statements of philosophy and goals are misleading guides to what actually happens in classrooms, and therefore best deposited in the least accessible fastnesses of the files, the converse is true at BBA. What the school's educators say and write about their philosophy and goals is the basis of today's lesson and tomorrow's lesson plan (pp. 38-39).

Religious instruction is most important in this school, followed by English. A one-year speech course is closely allied to the English program. Music is also important. All other subjects — mathematics, social studies, science, and others — are useful and interesting, but of secondary importance.

The teachers at Bethany are considered substitute parents. Therefore, they must model devotion to the church and separation from the world. They do so with conviction, even though the demands upon their non-teaching time is extraordinarily higher than that of the typical public school teacher — and with much less compensation. But without exception, they feel that it is easier to teach in a Christian school. Peshkin observes, "The teachers are at BBA and remain there because of their calling to serve the Lord in a Christian educational institution, not because of their inability to acquire work elsewhere."

A significant portion of the book describes students and what happens in their educational process. Peshkin reports that he expected those students who enrolled in a Christian school to be different from their public school peers. He learned that they do differ, but never completely. For example, BBA students delighted in classes that sidetracked from the subject, athletes performed academically in order to remain eligible for basketball, they tested first-year teachers, and their self-entertainment when the teacher wasn't present was the fun of all students. "In short, within the framework of the special school Christian educators have established, there is an ordinary school, as ordinary as acne and McDonald's yellow arches," Peshkin observed.

BBA does have its scorners too. ("Scorners" is the name attached by Peshkin to those who depart from Bethany's norms more than their mentors usually know, but so much less than their wordly peers as to hardly merit the name.) Some students do steal; some do get pregnant; some write profanity in library books. About a third of 60 students interviewed believed that teachers played favorites, especially with the children of Bethany's pastors, teachers, and administrative staff. A number of students rebel against the compulsion to do "Christian things." Indeed, Peshkin concluded, BBA's students are not mindless conformists.

By and large, Peshkin presents BBA in an objective framework, despite his own philosophical and religious variance with what he observed. He is to be commended for that. His concluding chapter, however, analyzes what he saw from his own perspective. He notes that Christian schools may spur public schools to change in ways that do not require a religious commitment — the commitment of teachers and students with attractive personal qualities, for example. He points out that the Christian school may relieve the public school of having to serve diverse masters. He states: "I do not believe that our typically diverse public schools can or should satisfy fully the needs and interests of the parents of all school-aged children. To do so reduces their operations to a level that, in not being repugnant to any, can satisfy no one" (p. 280). That is an uncomfortable statement to Christians, yet an acknowledgement of the realities of value education in the public schools of a pluralistic society. Only a Christian school can really design the kind of environment that produces Christian results.

Peshkin is concerned about the indoctrination in Christian schools like Bethany. He admits that indoctrination is not uncommon in public schools. But he suggests that the critical fact is that most public schools have built-in diversity in the heterogeneity of their students and teachers as well as their libraries. By contrast, the Christian school encourages its students to separate. He acknowledges that what BBA students do learn they learn well. But he adds, "The price they pay is what they do not become, what they cannot enjoy, what they fail to comprehend."

Finally, Peshkin discusses his personal reactions. He said that he experienced no bigotry at BBA. Yet, he felt intensely that fundamentalist Christians believe that Jews are doomed, imperfect, incomplete, and are not heard by God when they pray. He reacted negatively to the evangelistic intent of the church and school. He observed, "I confess to worrying that true believers may dismiss my precious right to dissent as the arrogance of unbelievers, an impediment in the path of Truth" (p. 290).

In regard to American society, Peshkin sees no basis for alarm in the activities of fundamentalist institutions such as Bethany's church and school. Yet he maintains his concern for the student's understanding of the pluralistic nature of American society, especially since the principle was never seriously held before the students.

Having said all, Peshkin concludes that Christian schools offer an alternative to the public schools. His final statement in the book clarifies his position: "Not soon, or ever, I trust, will we deem that the time has unmistakably come to fight fundamentalist Christian schools" (p. 299).

All in all, from my perspective, Peshkin did a service to the Christian school movement. He described a Christian school fairly and accurately, using a credible research method. He demonstrated that the school studied carries out its philosophy and achieves the outcomes it seeks. It provides a real contribution to the literature of the Christian school movement. — *Eleanor Daniel*, Professor of Christian Education, The Cincinnati Bible Seminary.

A HISTORY OF PRIVATE LIFE: I-FROM PAGAN ROME TO BYZANTIUM. Edited by Paul Veyne. Tr. Arthur Goldhammer. Cambridge, Massachusetts: The Belknap Press of Harvard University Press, 1987. Cloth, 670 pp., $29.50.

History tends to proclaim the public face of a former age. Yet much of what it records is the result of values and beliefs that emerged closer to the core of life in what is called "the private domain." The dynamics of private life are difficult enough to ascertain in contemporary times; nevertheless, the late Philippe Aries, a noted French historian and a member of the *Annales* school of history, pursued the history of private life for the world of scholarship. His vision, energy, and enthusiasm launched a monumental historical endeavor — a five-volume series, edited by himself and Georges Duby, covering the development of private lives over the course of 20 centuries. *A History of Private Life: From Pagan Rome to Byzantium*, originally published as *Historie de la vie Privée, vol. 1, De l'Emipre romain á l' an mil* in 1985, is the first volume of the series recently translated for English readers. As its editor, Paul Veyne, noted, the nature of this pioneering research into a hidden history represents a process of discovery more than a finished synthesis. Nevertheless, the results can only be described as stimulating and provocative.

The first volume consists of five parts written by various specialists. It includes "The Roman Empire" by Paul Veyne, "Late Antiquity" by Peter Brown, "Domestic Architecture in Roman Africa" by Yvon Thebert, "Early Middle Ages in the West" by Michel Rouche, and "Byzantium in the Tenth and Eleventh Centuries" by Evelyne Patlagean. The editors chose to present a series of well-focused and vibrant samplings that span the eight and one-half centuries, rather than an exhaustive, detailed treatment of the periods. This was fortunate for the lay reader.

Although each of the five parts is distinctive in its approach and style, the content continues to contribute remarkable insights into the developing character of private life. The topics include every facet of private life: bathing, birthing, work, leisure, slavery, economics, sexuality, family relationships, women, patrimony, dwelling space, virtues, beliefs, violence, and death. Both its universal relevance as well as its somewhat titillating aberrations hold the lay reader's interest.

Paul Veyne's description of the Roman Empire of pagan antiquity comprises a third of the volume giving details of private life organized around themes. The lasting impression is of individuals defined by the essentially public nature of life. With the emergence of Christianity and the triumph of Christian morality, Peter Brown shows some interesting shifts. The civic man whose allegiance is the city becomes the good Christian whose allegiance is the church. The rise of monasticism in the fourth century, he claims, "destroyed the particularity of the city," and the "deportment of the Christian" became that of the monk with all sorts of ramifications on private life and on public life. Michel Rouche's journey into life in the early middle ages completes a cycle that brings human beings through a violent era and results in the individuals who are increasingly independent of their environment. "Once fearful of the world, man had to learn contempt for the world before he could set forth to conquer it" (p. 549). Finally, Patlagean indicates the vast cultural differences in the meaning of private and public through an examination of Byzantium of the tenth and eleventh centuries.

The History of Private Life is an impressive, interesting, and intellectually challenging work. It is a work that will complement the materials in Robert Bellah's *Habits of the Heart* and raise again the question of the individual and community.

My criticisms of this fine work are few and offered with a certain reticence, since I am not that familiar with the methodology of the *Annales* school. Nevertheless, I thought some of the authors' interpretations appeared far more encompassing than the data represented warranted. Second, although the style of writing is primarily descriptive and narrative, occasionally an author addresses comments directly to the reader. These sometimes reflected certain assumptions, if not biases (see p. 119). Finally, some authors employed huge leaps in thought and in time. For example, in a discussion on work in ancient Rome, the author makes a fleeting reference to Aristotle and to Metternich and returns immediately to the Greeks and Romans. One is left with feeling some cognitive whiplash. But perhaps such references are merely the mark of the expert.

For the contemporary religious education theorist, *The History of Private Life* will provide numerous insights into the private, communal, and public dimensions of religious belief and practice. It offers a view of early Christianity from multiple angles within a larger cultural context. Moreover, it does so with a certain disinterest. In one sense, it serves to demythologize the life of early Christianity. And certainly Christianity is no less deserving than the gospels. However, I think one of the primary contributions of the work to the contemporary religious educationist will be its discussion of family and sexuality through the ages. These two topics have a certain vital relevance for religious education today. Because religious education is in the private sphere where family relationships dominate, because sexuality is a central concern of our age for multiple reasons, and because there is a growing public face of religion, *The History of Private Life* is an invaluable resource for religious educators. The good news is that it makes very interesting reading. — *Mary Kay Oosdyke*, Aquinas College, Grand Rapids, Michigan.

DYNAMICS OF CREATIVITY: FOR ARTISTS AND LOVERS OF ART. By Peter Fingesten. Bristol, Ind.: Wyndham Hall Press, 1987. Paper, 53 pp., $7.95.

At first glance, one could wonder what purpose a book by an artist written for "artists and lovers of art" could have for those in the field of religious education. The wonder continues when one opens the pages of this little book. Instead of a conceptual or theoretical treatise on the dynamics of creativity, or an abstract guide on how to acquire or develop creativity, we find a collection of "aphorisms" (as the author calls them), short statements or maxims that Fingesten has gleaned from his own years as an artist and sculptor.

While loosely grouped into three sections entitled Art, Artists, and Drips and Splashes, the statements themselves are spread across the pages in what appears to be a random fashion much like multiple colors of paint that have been spattered with no apparent pattern onto a blank canvas. One is continually caught off guard by unpredictable statements such as "Since you cannot address a work of art with a verbal question, consider your question the answer"; "Pull yourself up, not by your bootstraps, but by your imagination"; "Art pinches some of its creators like too-tight shoes. When they loosen them to be more comfortable, they will discover that they cannot walk any more"; and "Don't be tempted to psychoanalyze your creative process while working, otherwise you will lose both yourself as well as the work in progress instead of losing yourself *in* your work." This book is read in fits and starts as one ponders the meaning of each new surprise.

But just as those spatters of color on a blank canvas can begin to take shape and form as we pause to ponder them, so too this book begins to take shape and form as one spends time with it. Fingesten is not asking us to think about the dynamics of creativity but to experience them as we read his book. He believes the creative person looks for the unusual, will "create new idea-collages from pre-existing elements and surprise us and himself with novel solutions." He says, "Since we only see what our culture permits us to see, we must partially reject it and borrow one foreign eye." His is that "foreign eye" bringing new awareness. And that awareness is at the heart of the creative process. As he points out, "The quality of one's paintings or sculptures does not increase with one's intelligence, but with one's awareness."

Let us now return to our original concern: What purpose could this book serve for the religious educator? In recent years there has been a call for a new vision of religious education, particularly of teaching as it occurs in the church. In response to the technological mindset that seems to influence much of what happens in teaching, voices like Mary Boys and Maria Harris are challenging us to conceive of teaching in artistic terms, to begin with the mystery and creativity that is at the heart of teaching. If one conceives of teaching as an art, a creative act, then Fingesten's "drips and splashes," the surprises that await us in the pages of this book, will challenge our own creative thinking, will invite us to explore the processes that lead to and accompany the creation of any work of art, including the work of teaching. Such creative activity seems to me to be at the heart of what religious education is all about. — *Karen Tye*, Associate Professor of Christian Education, American Baptist Seminary of the West, Berkeley, CA.

EMBRACING CONTRARIES: EXPLORATIONS IN LEARNING AND TEACHING. By Peter Elbow. New York and Oxford: Oxford University Press, 1986. Cloth, 314 pp., $19.95.

Maxine Greene, well-known teacher and author, speaks of teaching as encompassing "multiple small uncertainties." Peter Elbow develops her theme in his exploration of "contrary" elements involved in teaching: free-wheeling creativity and tough-minded criticism, judicial assessment and empathetic understanding, obligations to one's students — being their ally — and obligations to knowledge and society — being "enemies" of students.

His book rests on a view of rationality as the interaction between careful and conscious inferences and "careless" thinking involving association, digression, and relinquishment of control. Elbow maintains that "thinking in contraries usually holds us back because it so often leads us to stalemate or warfare; yet, if well managed, it is the very source of progress" (p. 54). It is this thesis that provides a loose theme for the 12 essays collected in the volume.

Several of Elbow's essays bear wisdom and relevance for religious educators. His "Methodological Doubting and Believing: Contraries in Believing" insightfully names that dynamic involved in dialogue with texts and other interpreters. "The Pedagogy of the Bamboozled" offers a refreshing perspective on Paulo Freire, and "Cooking: The Interaction of Conflicting Elements" provides a seasoned writer's perspicuity on writing.

Other essays are interesting, sometimes challenging, and always candid. This anthology, however, is constituted by essays selected over 20 years; most of them have been published elsewhere and some are specific recommendations for particular situations (e.g., competency-based education, analyses of another's teaching). Not surprisingly, then, *Embracing Contraries* has a few contradictions of its own. Its author is widely known as a writing teacher, yet the volume is not carefully edited for repetitions and for exclusive language. Further, there is no recognition of the role of the computer in composition and revision; Elbow has not updated his advice on "desperation writing" to include the contribution of word processing. And one wonders whether "embracing contraries" is a theme rationalizing a loosely unified volume.

In the final analysis, I found this volume disappointing. Admittedly, I had high expectations of a writer passionate about teaching. Elbow *is* perceptive and writes with flair. But he owes the teaching profession not an anthology of previously published work but a unified and polished piece. I suggest Kenneth Eble's *Craft of Teaching* as a model for him. — *Mary C. Boys, S.N.J.M.*, Associate Professor of Theology and Religious Education, Boston College.

WHEN CHILDREN SUFFER: A SOURCEBOOK FOR MINISTRY WITH CHILDREN IN CRISIS. By Andrew Lester, ed. Philadelphia: The Westminster Press, 1987. Cloth, 216 pp., $14.95.

Lester has presented a sequel to his *Pastoral Care with Children in Crisis*, a rich collection of resource chapters by practicing professionals to help the pastor minister to the school-age child whose parents are divorcing, who is facing illness or loss, who is disabled or abused, or who is under severe stress.

The book is divided into three sections. Part I provides an overview of the elementary child's development and what she or he needs from caring adults; Part II, the core of the work, contains specific chapters on particular crises by chaplains, social workers, and pastors reflecting their expertise in each area; Part III contains helps for pastoral assessment and referral for families with children in difficulty. Throughout the work the riches of the faith are brought to bear on each issue in a way that speaks to the child's developmental level and experience.

"Crisis" is defined by Olle Jane Sahler as a "short term and self limited state" characterized by immediacy and urgency during which intervention is particularly salient. It is difficult to see how this definition of crisis fits the disabled child for whom the condition of sensory impairment constitutes a long-term or even lifetime difficulty. The chronically ill child would fit into the same category. The rationale for inclusion of the disabled child may be that integrating that child into the religious community or educational setting frequently results in an immediate crisis for churches. A more careful reading of other chapters develops the concept presented by Sahler in the introductory section that adults' and childrens' perceptions of what constitutes a crisis may differ greatly. Andrew Puckett picks up this theme in his chapter on the bereaved child. The loss of a pet or a move may be as devastating as the death of a family member. Although all nine chapters in Part II deal with important issues confronted by pastors in their ministry with children and families, it is hard to see how they all fit into a definition of crisis, which is described as short-term and immediate.

Granted the validity of the chapter themes for ministry with children in trouble, the major emphases permeating the book are valuable. High priority is given to listening to children as the key to establishing the relationship between pastor and child. A further recommendation is meeting the child in a setting where he or she feels more comfortable — home, playground, or children's classroom. Strategies for utilizing toys, books, or personal stories are promoted. A wealth of concrete examples for discussing how faith and biblical themes impact each crisis are offered from the first-hand clinical experience of the authors. Finally, "Further Reading" at the end of each chapter provides additional resources for the adult helping children, whether for the pastor, a parent, or church school teacher who needs assistance in understanding a particular issue.

Although the major focus of this book is the pastoral relationship with a child in a one-on-one setting, the content can be helpful to educators who become engaged in pastoral care of children. The chapter on the abused child raises the concern of how that child fits into the religious community. The chapter on the disabled child assists with how the sensory or physically impaired child may be included in the local church's program as full participants. Probably the most salient chapter deals with how the learning disabled or hyperactive child causes problems in many a children's program because his or her (though most frequently his) condition is not adequately understood by lay leaders. Valuable suggestions and mandates to educators are the hallmark of this chapter, which also promotes the need for preparing peers and other congregation members to deal with this particular child.

The limitation of this book for educators is its lack of program material to help *groups* of teachers or children face these critical problems in the church. A work that expands the scope of treatment of such timely topics beyond pastoral care would be a valuable asset to the professional literature. Still, this collection provides valuable information about children who suffer and a strong advocacy message on their behalf, which includes the extended family and utilization of community resources. — *Mary Anne Fowlkes*, Presbyterian School of Christian Education.

BRIEFLY NOTED

AIDS: A MANUAL FOR PASTORAL CARE. By Ronald H. Sunderland and Earl E. Shelp. Philadelphia: The Westminster Press, 1987. Paper, 76 pp., $6.95. Medical facts, guides to grief recognition and responses, approaches to pastoral care of people with AIDS, and ethical issues shape the content of this short book. Educators may be interested in the three cases, suitable for class discussion, that form the final chapter. — R. H. C.

ALCOHOL AND THE FAMILY: A COMPREHENSIVE BIBLIOGRAPHY. Compiled by Grace M. Barnes and Diane K. Augustino. Westport, CT: Greenwood Press, 1987. Cloth, 461 pp., $49.95. The most comprehensive listing available of resources in this area. Such issues as family-related stresses of aging, socialization of children, and family violence are fully documented. A sound research tool for the religious educator; a *must* for the religious education library reference section. — R. H. C.

COLLABORATIVE MINISTRY: SKILLS AND GUIDELINES. By Loughlan Sofield, ST; and Carroll Juliano, SHCJ. Notre Dame: Ave Maria Press, 1987. Paper, 134 pp., $5.95. A practical approach to shared ministry. Chapters on group leadership, conflict, and group leadership may provide the practitioner with helpful guidelines. — R. H. C.

COMFORT AND PROTEST: REFLECTIONS ON THE APOCALYPSE OF JOHN OF PATMOS. By Allan A. Boesak. Philadelphia, Westminster Press, 1987. Paper, 144 pp., $7.95. Forged on the anvil of personal experience of apartheid, with its resultant oppression and pain, Boesak holds up a ray of hope through this helpful study of the Apocalypse. Crisply written, and deeply personal, the text allows us to view how John's message might engage our current Caesars. — A. B. L.

THE DEVIL'S OTHER STORYBOOK. By Natalie Babbitt. New York: Michael di Capua Books, 1987. Cloth, 82 pp., $10.95. Whatever happened to the devil in the religious education of children? The question is especially worth pondering in light of this collection of stories about a devil who is portrayed as a practical joker, and a sort of lovable moral educator. Superbly written, this highly popular book is worthly of careful and reflective reading. — R. H. C.

THE GREATEST ADVENTURE, STORIES FROM THE BIBLE: THE NATIVITY. By Joseph Barbera and William Hanna, executive producers. Hanna-Barbera, 1986. VHS, approximately 30 minutes, $19.95. One of seven tapes that depict biblical stories through animated cartoon figures. — R. H. C.

INSIDE AMERICA'S CHRISTIAN SCHOOLS. By Paul F. Parsons. Macon: Mercer University Press, 1987. Paper, 193 pp., $12.95. Based on field research conducted in thirty states, this book provides the reader with a general "feel" for the current non-Catholic Christian school movement. Guided by the assumption that the contemporary Christian school movement is "a vehement rejection of contemporary America," Parsons makes a useful contribution to comparative religious education studies. — R. H. C.

INTRODUCTION TO CHRISTIAN EDUCATION. By Eleanor Daniel, John W. Wade, and Charles Gresham. Cincinnati: Standard Publishing, 1987. Paper, 352 pp., $6.95. An updated version of the 1980 edition. This is a representative introductory text for conservative evangelical Christian educators that equates Christian education with church education. Its scripture index is of special interest. — R. H. C.

LORD, TEACH ME TO PRAY. By Jean-Guy Paradis. Mystic: Twenty-Third Publications, 1987. Paper, 237 pp., $9.95. English translation of the French original, this book is a practical guide based on a three stage sequence. Prayers for Advent and Christmas/Lent and Easter may be especially useful resources for the religious educator. — R. H. C.

PARENTS ON SUCCESSFUL PARENTING. By John J. Envoy. Kansas City: Sheed & Ward, 1987. Paper, 129 pp., $7.95. Do we really need another book on parenting? This one is different in that in it we hear the actual voices of parents who in the author's view have been successful. Selection was limited to two-parent, Catholic families. The book contains a wealth of commonsense wisdom that many who are parents will appreciate. — D. J. H.

THE PEACEMAKER. By Myron S. Augsburger. Nashville: Abingdon Press, 1987. Paper, 108 pp., $9.95. Drawing from the perspective of an evangelical pastor and teacher from the Anabaptist tradition this work focuses on the ethical aspect of a Christological faith. The ethic is one of peace based upon the life and person of Jesus Christ. The implications of this ethic for several areas of modern life are examined. — C. R. M.

PRAYER AND OUR CHILDREN: PASSING ON THE TRADITION. By Mary Terese Donze, A.S.C. Notre Dame: Ave Maria Press, 1987. Paper, 96 pp., $3.95. Donze presents a case for reclaiming the traditional devotional practices of the Catholic Church, ranging from the rosary to grace before meals, for to-day's children. Providing many practical suggestions, this little book would be of primary interest to those concerned with the spiritual formation of children within the Catholic faith. — D. J. H.

THE PROPHETHOOD OF ALL BELIEVERS. By James Luther Adams. Edited by George K. Beach. Boston: Beacon Press, 1987. Paper, 324 pp., $12.95. Reflecting the breadth and depth of Adams' work in the field of social ethics over five decades, these essays portray the views and development of one of America's foremost liberal thinkers. If one discerns that faith must lead to moral action, this volume should be required reading. — A. B. L.

PUBLIC SCHOOLS IN HARD TIMES: THE GREAT DEPRESSION AND RECENT YEARS. By David Tyack, Robert Lowe, and Elisabeth Hansot. Cambridge: Harvard University Press, 1984. Cloth, 267 pp., $20.00. Although no overt connection between religious education and public education is made in this book, the authors provide the religious education historian with the public educational context along side of which religious education curriculum resources and programs were being formed. The book may also provide clues to the current rise of non-Catholic Christian private schools. — R. H. C.

RELIGION AND VIOLENCE. By Robert McAfee Brown. Philadelphia: The Westminster Press, 1987. Paper, 114 pp., $8.95. The second edition of the book with a new introduction by the author. The introduction contains an outline of seven concerns about religion and violence that could be used as discussion guides for the book in an adult education setting. — R. H. C.

THE ROLE OF THE THEOLOGIAN. By Monika K. Hellwig. Kansas City: Sheed & Ward, 1987. Paper, 44 pp., $2.95. Responding to the turmoil currently surrounding the role of theologians in the Catholic Church, Hellwig suggests that they have a number of necessary parts to play — Myth-Maker, Fool, Comforter, Builder, Archivist, Critic, Archeologist, and Ghost. An insightful discussion of benefit to all who are interested in the theological task. — D. J. H.

TO START A WORK: THE FOUNDATIONS OF PROTESTANT MISSION IN KOREA (1884-1919). By Martha Huntley. Seoul, Korea: Presbyterian Church of Korea, 1987. paper, 660 pp., n.p. This is an informal historical study of the nature of early missionary activity in Korea. A chapter that focuses on American Christian education models in a Confucian society, "An Elephant by the Tail," will be of special interest to those seeking a better understanding of the relationship between culture and religious education. — R. H. C.

WORLD SPIRITUALITY: AN ENCYCLOPEDIC HISTORY OF THE RELIGIOUS QUEST. Edited by Ewert Cousins. Vol. 17, CHRISTIAN SPIRITUALITY: HIGH MIDDLE AGES AND REFORMATION. Edited by Jill Raitt, Bernard McGinn, and John Meyendorff. New York: Crossroad Publishing, 1987. Cloth, 479 pp., $49.50. This second volume in a trilogy written on Christian Spirituality covers the period from 1150 to 1600, exploring the groups, movements, themes and influential figures of all major traditions. A solid overview of a crucial period, the book should serve well as a text or resource for study of this era. — A. B. L.

Books Received January, 1988

Adam Ford, UNIVERSE

Stephan Rowan, WORDS FROM THE CROSS

Mark Smith, PSALMS

John Heil, PAUL'S LETTER TO THE ROMANS

Fritz Kunkel, CONTINUOUS CREATIONS

Edmund Flood, ALL IS OURS